To Tommi

Christmas 94

Love: from your dad

It's a Funny Old Life

It's a Funny Old Life

JIMMY GREAVES

ARTHUR BARKER
A division of Weidenfeld Publishers Ltd
London

To Irene, for everything.

Published in Great Britain by
George Weidenfeld & Nicolson Limited
91 Clapham High Street
London SW4 7TA

ISBN 0 213 85002 8

Printed in Great Britain by
Butler & Tanner Ltd, Frome and London

Contents

Illustrations

The story so far

My life has been like a football match with two distinct halves. During the half-time interval I was drunk out of my head. I was the footballing legend who became legless.

I told the story of the first half of my life – the international footballer turned hopeless alcoholic – in a book called *This One's On Me*.*

If anything, the second half has so far been even more hectic and demanding than the first. It's certainly been funnier.

You join me where *This One's On Me* left off, with me divorced, living alone in a one-roomed rented flat, and earning my daily bread by selling ladies' sweaters.

It is six months after I had stood up at an Alcoholics Anonymous meeting and declared: 'My name is Jimmy G. I am a professional footballer, and I am an alcoholic.'

This is not a Kiss and Tell book, more like Kick and Tell! I have told the story with the invaluable assistance and memory jogging from my writing partner Norman Giller. I hope you have as much fun reading it as I've had living it.

***This One's On Me* was originally published by Arthur Barker Limited in 1979.

CHAPTER ONE

The comeback

The second half of my life started as the first half had finished, with me in a position that was all too familiar: on my knees, head over the toilet and being as sick as a dog. It was the spring of 1979 and I was about to make my first public appearance since admitting that I was an alcoholic. Downstairs in the London Weekend Television studio Russell Harty was waiting to interview me on the *Russell Harty Plus* show. Upstairs I was throwing up. It's a funny old life!

For the past five years I had been a hopeless drunk fully accustomed to the indignity and degradation of vomiting. I had humiliated myself on some of the best carpets money could buy, as well as in the gutter. But this time I had not been drinking. I was sick with nerves.

God, what I could do with a drink now. There's nothing wrong with me that a glass or three of vodka could not put right. What the hell am I doing here? Why do I want to go on television and make a fool of myself in front of millions of people?

A concerned researcher for the Russell Harty programme knocked on the door of the hospitality room loo. 'Are you all right, Mr Greaves? You're wanted in the studio.'

I fully intended to say that I felt unwell, and that I could not go through with the show. But the inner voice that recovering alcoholics get to know so well started to attack me.

Running away again, Greavsie. You're going to let down the publishers of your book who arranged this interview. You're going to let down Russell Harty. The same old Greavsie. You've done nothing but let people down for the past five years. Your wife – your ex-wife, that is – your kids, your business colleagues, your friends. And, most of all, yourself.

I managed to shame myself sufficiently into facing up to the fact that I *had* to go through with the interview, otherwise I knew that my running away would lead me in only one direction: back to the bottle.

As I returned to the hospitality room the other guest on the show arrived, best-selling author Arthur Hailey. We were introduced and he told me that he was glad that I was on first because it would give him more time to compose himself and get over his nerves. It was my first realisation that just about everybody suffers from a bout of nerves before facing the dreaded television camera.

A programme assistant guided me through a maze of corridors and downstairs to the studio where I was about to meet Russell Harty for the first time in my life. I was visibly shaking with tension as I stood inside the door waiting to make my entrance on to the set in front of a studio audience of a couple of hundred people. It was like a return of the boozer's shakes I had got to know so well. I was still having to fight the urge to turn and run away as I watched on a monitor while Russell read my introduction from an Autocue. It went like this. . .

'My first guest tonight is a man who has been an idol of millions, a footballer *par excellence* who during a distinguished playing career rewrote the goal-scoring record books. But he is here this evening not to talk about football but about the nightmare he has lived since retiring from the game he graced with such skill and flair. In an astonishingly frank book he has confessed to being an alcoholic. It is, of course, the one and only Jimmy Greaves, but before we meet him let us take a look at some of the goals he scored that lifted him into the land of footballing legend . . .'

Flickering on to the screen came old black and white shots of a young, nimble, quick-as-a-flash footballer banging in goals from all angles. There were goals for Chelsea, goals for Tottenham, goals for England and – real collectors' items these – even goals for West Ham. So much had happened to me since those summertime days of my life that I found it difficult to identify with the jinking footballer to whom goals seemed to come so effortlessly.

Suddenly a floor manager was signalling me forward on to the set, and Russell Harty was announcing me as if I were somebody special. My confidence was so low that I felt anything but special. I just wanted to get the hell out of there. If you had told me that less than six years later I would be back in that self-same studio co-hosting a national networked show with Ian St John I would have accused you of being more pissed than I'd ever been.

Anyway, Russell Harty loomed over me as he stood to greet me. He was much bigger than he looked on the screen, and the first thing I was aware of as he clasped my shaking hand is that he was wringing wet with perspiration. He was leaking bubbles of sweat through the heavy make-up on his face, and I became almost transfixed by a large pearl of perspiration that was rolling down his nose, and I watched it drop on to his extra-wide top lip where it formed a small pool. Within seconds of being invited to sit alongside him I realised why he was in such a state. It was sweltering under the studio lights, and both Russell and I were dressed in heavy lounge suits.

After a preamble about the goals we had just seen – with me admitting that it had all seemed a lifetime ago – Russell got down to the nitty gritty. He had an odd yet effective way of interviewing. Just as he seemed to be going all round the houses with his line of interrogation he would suddenly hit you between the eyes with a blunt question. 'It is true, is it not,' he asked, 'that after a football career that brought you much fame and not a little fortune you admit to having become a helpless alcoholic?'

It was the moment I had been dreading since agreeing to do the interview. It was one thing admitting at a meeting of Alcoholics Anonymous that I was an alcoholic, and confessing it to a ghostwriter to be put down in black and white in a book. But to openly declare to millions of television viewers that I was an alcoholic was going to be, so I thought, one of the hardest things I had ever done in my life.

But Russell had got me so relaxed with what was clearly a genuine interest in my problem that I found myself talking quite easily about the horrors of my drinking habit. I told him about how my consumption had reached two bottles of vodka a day, plus countless pints of beer; and how my drinking had cost me my marriage, my business, my friends, my home and my self-respect.

I explained that I was opening up my heart not only to publicise my book, *This One's On Me*, but also because I honestly wanted to try to help anybody facing the curse of the drink problem to believe that they could beat it.

'Are you sure that *you've* beaten it?' asked Russell in that disarming way of his.

I shrugged. 'I will always be an alcoholic,' I told him. 'The important thing is that I must be a *non-drinking* alcoholic – a drunk who doesn't drink. The only way I can do that is not have a drink today. That's the simple rule I must follow for the rest of my life. "Today I must be sober. Just for today." I am in the early stages of recovery from what is a serious illness. And today I am not drinking.'

Russell was just about to dig deeper into my drinking history when the floor manager started waving his arms about like a tic-tac man. He pointed to the boom mike that had come down towards us like the blade of a guillotine.

'There's something wrong with the mike,' said the floor manager.

'It looks as if it's got brewer's droop to me,' I said.

Russell listened to instructions in his earpiece from his director. 'Sorry about this, Jim,' he said, 'but we'll have to stop recording while they fix it. We'll pick up where we left off when we get the go-ahead.'

The break lasted twenty minutes during which I had a quiet conversation with Russell that was far more fascinating than the one we had just recorded.

I started him off by apologising for my hands shaking. 'It's nothing to do with my booze problem,' I said. 'It's just that I was a bag of nerves when I first came on to the set.'

Russell wiped away a pool of perspiration gathered on his top lip. 'This sweat isn't just caused by the heat, you know,' he said. 'I am petrified before the start of any of my shows. But I find that I need to be in a nervous state to motivate myself. The day I relax before going in front of a camera is the day that I will become complacent and not perform to the best of my ability. Nearly everybody in television, certainly those in front of the cameras, live on their nerves. You show me somebody who is not nervous when the red light is about to go on and I will show you somebody who bores the viewers.'

'It was the same for me in my peak playing days,' I said. 'I was as nervous as a rabbit at harvest time before a match, but once the first whistle had been blown I would relax and get on with the game. You would be surprised at how many players are physically sick before matches.'

'Did you start drinking to calm your nerves?' Russell asked.

'No. I never ever drank immediately before a match. For me, a good drink was the reward I promised myself *after* a game.

In the middle of a match I would lick my lips at the prospect of a pint when it was all over. Drinking was never a problem to me when I was playing League football. It was when I jacked in the game that it got out of control.'

Russell then leant forward and spoke in a confidential way as if passing me a secret.

'I really admire the way that you've stood up and confessed to your problem,' he said. 'So many people refuse to admit that they drink too much. You'd be shocked at how many people inside the world of television have the problem, but without admitting it. I hope they see this programme because it might encourage them to take a good look at themselves. In fact, when we re-start the interview I'll ask you how people with the problem should, one, recognise it, and, two, set about conquering it.'

When Russell put the questions on air I trotted out the stock AA doctrine, because I could not – and still can't – think of a better way of tackling the menace of drink. 'You recognise that you have a problem,' I said, 'when you start to drink because you *have* to and not just because you *want* to. And your problem is serious when you are drinking to the detriment of your work and to the exclusion and distress of your family and friends.'

'Right,' said Russell. 'Now how about conquering it? What can anybody do if he or she recognises they have a problem?'

'They have already taken the first most important step if they accept that they have a problem,' I told him. 'Speaking from my own personal experience, I would urge that the best thing to do is contact Alcoholics Anonymous. They would be warmly welcomed and encouraged to follow the three stages of rehabilitation – one, admission . . . two, adjustment . . . three, achievement. I'm into the early stages of adjustment after clearing the biggest hurdle which is admitting to be an alcoholic.'

I felt like a released prisoner when the interview finally finished and could not wait to get back to the hospitality room for a drink. I felt everybody's eyes boring into me as I went to the bar and placed my order . . . for a large, iced glass of Perrier water. Arthur Hailey, whose books such as *Airport, Hotel* and *The Moneychangers* have been worldwide best sellers, shook my hand. 'Congratulations on an excellent interview,' he said. 'There are a lot of my friends who could do with listening to you. They drink too much but just won't admit to it. It's good to see somebody in the public eye honest enough to talk so openly about what is a major problem.'

Unfortunately there were quite a few members of Alcoholics Anonymous who did not think I had done such a good job. I received a lot of stick for allegedly betraying the AA code of anonymity. But I had a clear conscience. The fact that I had a drink problem and was an AA member had been blown by Fleet Street. It was the price of being famous and once it was out in the open I decided to get my story across to try to help others. There was no risk whatsoever of my revealing any of the facts I had heard about fellow members during AA meetings. I owed AA too much to want to damage their principles.

Some years later I met Russell Harty at an awards ceremony and reminded him that he had given me the first chance to come back into the public spotlight. By then he was a mega chat show star with the BBC, and I was established as something of a screen personality in my own right.

'I have watched every moment of your progress,' he told me. 'I remember the way your hands shook on the day that I interviewed you, and to be perfectly honest I did not see how you were going to be able to beat your problem. I shall write an article about you in my *Sunday Times* column. I'll call it *The Man Who Came Back*.'

I never did see the article, and within six months Russell was dead. He had taken a terrible hounding from the Press over matters in his private life, and the killer disease that he picked up led to all sorts of spiteful innuendo. You can only take as you find, and to me Russell Harty was a warm, gifted and caring man with a sensitive nature that seemed somehow out of place in what can be the cut-throat world of television.

I will always remember Russell with gratitude as one of the people who helped me make my comeback. But the person who has to take most of the credit for getting me back on to a sober track is a woman. My ex-wife, Irene.

Immediately after my appearance on the Russell Harty show I drove myself home in my flash, yellow Jaguar XJ6. I was selling ladies' sweaters for a living and hardly had two pennies to rub together, but the car was the one luxury that I was determined to hang on to while everything was being sold around me to clear debts incurred at the peak – or rather, depths – of my drinking disease (and a disease is exactly what it was).

Home was a tiny one-room rented flat in Wanstead on the outskirts of East London. But if home is where the heart is then I really belonged a dozen or so miles down the road at Upminster in Essex where Irene was living with our four kids – Lynn, 21, Mitzi, 18, Danny, 17 and Andrew, 14. We had been married for twenty years when Irene decided to divorce me, or, as she put it, the stranger that I had become. She just could not take any more of my violent swings of mood brought on by my alcohol addiction.

When I had woken up in a Brentwood mental hospital in the winter of 1978 after a wild bender I was told by doctors that if I did not stop drinking I would be in my grave within a year. That was when Irene decided the time had come for drastic action. She knew I was completely out of control and saw divorce as a last-ditch attempt to shock me to my senses. I felt as if my world had caved in on me.

The divorce became absolute in the spring of 1979 and, thanks to the mess that I had made of things, Irene was having to sell our beautiful house that overlooked Upminster golf course. I was welcome there at weekends on the strict understanding that I behaved myself. Just a hint of having had a drink and I would have been out on my ear. Meantime, Irene was arranging to buy a smaller, much more modest house half a mile away. I had cost her a dream home, and years later I was able to calculate that the sale of that immaculate house at a time when the market was stagnant had hit us in the pocket for a nice few grand.

Well done, Greavsie.

While I had been drinking myself to ruin and damaging business interests that I had built up with my brother-in-law, Tom, Irene had found an escape route from the misery that I had made of her life. She showed the strength of character that was totally lacking in me, and qualified as a State Registered Nurse. By working at a local hospital she was able to concentrate her mind on something other than my self-inflicted crisis. To add to her burden, Irene had to get power of attorney over my business affairs to stop my headlong dive towards bankruptcy. My brain was too pickled for me to be able to sort things out myself.

During all these traumas I was still managing to play football. It was seven years since I had foolishly ended my League career at the age of 31, but I had found a happy base in the Southern

League with Barnet for whom I played between mindless benders.

Irene's decision to divorce me was just the jolt that I needed. Suddenly I had a target in life – to win back the woman I loved. I wanted her back more than anything in the world, and the only chance I had of doing that was if I stopped drinking. It was the greatest motivation I could possibly have had.

My big chance to show that I had at least *started* to beat the bottle came when my eldest daughter, Lynn, announced that she was getting married. Both Irene and I – and, of course, our kids – wanted Lynn to go down the aisle with a united family behind her. As we started making plans for the wedding it became a good excuse for me to spend more time at my old home, and gradually I managed to win Irene's confidence. She had been so used over the past nightmare six or seven years to seeing me as a puppet of alcohol that she had lost all faith in my ability to beat the sickness that comes out of a bottle like a genie and then gobbles you up like a monster. I had lost her trust, but I knew that, deep down, I had not lost her love.

We started seeing each other on a regular basis like a young courting couple, and as we repaired the bridges between us I was able to show Irene that I really meant it about beating my booze problem. The only thing that had ever come between us was the bottle, and now I was kicking that into touch.

Three months after our divorce had become absolute – a worthless piece of paper from which only the legal beagles profited – we were back living together. Loving in sin, we called it. We celebrated with a 'honeymoon' in France, which made up for not having had one the first time around when we were both eighteen. Back in those days I was just starting out on my career as a professional footballer with Chelsea, and we got married in the middle of the football season which was frowned on by the old pros in the game. But Irene and I have never gone in for convention. If you see a crowd of people going thataway, the couple walking hand-in-hand in the opposite direction will doubtless be Irene and me. And that's how it has been with our new life together. We go our own way, and turn a blind eye, a deaf ear and a couple of fingers to the tongue-clicking rumour-mongers, who cannot understand why we don't tie the knot again. We will get re-married when we feel the time is right. But it will be because we want to do it, not because of pointed fingers or whispered gossip. A newspaper offered to pay all expenses for us to fly abroad and get re-married in return for exclusive photographs. Thanks, but no thanks. When we do it we will do it quietly, privately and romantically. Meanwhile, we are perfectly content loving in sin.

When we returned from our French 'honeymoon,' I faced the big 'all-eyes-on-Jim' test of giving Lynn away, and then helping Irene host the big bash afterwards. A lot of the people at the wedding had been so accustomed to seeing me the worse for drink that I am sure they half expected me to fall flat on my face. But there was no prouder Dad than old Greavsie that day in June 1979 when I led the radiant Lynn up the aisle. She looked a picture, as did her mum – the woman whom I had won back. Mitzi was a beautiful bridesmaid, and Danny and Andy appeared remarkably grown up in their roles as church ushers. Even if I say it myself, it was a great show by the Greavsies, and to be together as a family again gave me one of the most warming feelings of satisfaction I have ever experienced. And it was all down to the remarkable Irene.

At the reception afterwards I was in charge of the toasts. There was enough booze around to have opened a pub, and in the bad old days I would have been swimming in it long before we reached the speeches. But I filled my champagne glass with Perrier water, and toasted the bride and groom with a speech that was delivered with emotion and humour that owed nothing to the bottle.

The fact that Lynn's marriage did not last is another story, and I would just like to briefly zap forward in time to nail a lie. When Lynn and her husband had their well-publicised break-up three years after the wedding it was reported that I had gone after him with a seven-iron golf club. Actually it was a five-iron. Just to put the record straight, I took the golf club with me only to force an entry into my daughter's house where my gorgeous granddaughter, Victoria, was waiting to be reunited with her mother. I had a bit of a barney with her now ex-husband, but it was all ironed out (pun intended) after a few words with the police, and everything has since been settled.

I had given my daughter away, and I was delighted to take her back. Lynn and Victoria are inseparable and seeing them together brings me enormous pleasure. The newspapers reporting on my golf swing naturally referred to my drinking history, and the impression given was that I had acted while under the influence. The truth is that I was as sober as a judge . . . which triggers an anecdote that is worth repeating here as a relief from the traumas of my funny old life: F.E. (Frederick) Smith, who was later Lord Birkenhead, was one of the wittiest barristers ever to don the wig and gown. During an Old Bailey trial he referred to one of the witnesses as being 'as drunk as a judge at the time of the offence'. At this point the red-robed judge gave a forced cough and interrupted. 'I believe you mean to say as drunk as a lord, not as drunk as a judge,' he boomed. F.E. Smith bowed to the bench and said, 'As your lordship pleases.'

Sorry about that. Now where was I? Oh yes, back with Irene, thank God. From the moment we were reunited, I got a lot of my old confidence and bounce back and I began to get my life on to a sensible course. *The Sun* newspaper gave me a weekly platform for my views on football, for which I will always be grateful to the then Sports Editor Frank Nicklin, who had faith in me when many others preferred to look the other way if I was anywhere in sight. In fact it was for *The Sun* football team that I played my last game. I felt a twinge in the area of the back that had troubled me throughout my career, and I decided that, at 39, the time had come to hang up the old shooting boots for good. A week earlier I had played my final serious game, which was the testimonial match for my old adversary Ron 'Chopper' Harris at Stamford Bridge where my footballing career had started twenty-five years earlier. I played alongside a useful centre-forward called Ian Botham, who could have made quite an impact as a professional footballer but for deciding to concentrate on cricket. When I changed alongside Both in the dressing-room I discovered just why he is nicknamed Guy. What a physique! He is built like a brick outhouse (that's me being polite), and when he used his enormous strength on the football pitch defenders bounced off him as if they had run into a wall. I have always been a Botham fan, and rate him the greatest cricketer of my lifetime. Only George Best has had to cope with the sort of microscopic media attention that Both has had to endure. We know what the pressure did to George (one of the few boozers who could have drunk me under the table at my peak), but Both has had the character to battle his way through the poisonous publicity and has somehow managed to survive with his sanity intact.

Anyway, Both was my last playing partner and once I had

made the decision not to kick another ball I contented myself with watching my two sons, Danny and Andy, trying to make a go of it as professionals with Southend United. Both of them, particularly Danny, would have made it but for being haunted by their name. Every report I read on Danny used to start, 'Danny Greaves, son of...' It was too big a burden to be constantly compared with somebody who had been lucky enough to have been blessed with a natural gift for banging the ball into the net. Both Danny and Andrew dropped down into non-League football where they play for pleasure, which is the way the game was meant to be played. Danny, player-manager of Witham Town, is now on the Southend payroll on the administration side, and still has playing ambitions following a nasty injury. Andy is 'something in the City,' a real grafter with the sort of bubbling personality that will carry him through all of life's crises. They – along with their two sisters – are a credit to Irene, who worked wonders to hold the family together while I was taking a blurred view of the world through the bottom of a glass.

My income from *The Sun* meant I was able to return my stock of ladies' sweaters to knitwear fashion supplier Geoffrey Green, who had generously helped me keep life and limb together in the hard times when I was just coming out of my drunken stupor. For a year I had been ducking and diving for a living like a real-life version of Del Boy Trotter, the Cockney spiv so brilliantly portrayed by David Jason in *Only Fools and Horses*. The only difference was that I was driving around in a Jaguar rather than a Robin Reliant, but the colour was the same as Del Boy's yellow three wheeler and my goods were sometimes as dodgy as his. They didn't exactly fall off the back of a lorry, but I often had to obtain them by using craft and cunning rather than traditional business methods.

When I see some of the episodes of *Only Fools and Horses* I wonder if that master scriptwriter John Sullivan was looking over my shoulder. I used to handle the bulk buying and selling of anything from ladies' sweaters to sports shoes, cashed in on the skateboarding craze, bought and sold parcels of 'quality' goods direct from Taiwan and knocked out at giveaway prices any bankrupt stock I could lay my hands on. Most of my business was done as a go-between for warehouse wholesalers and market traders, marvellous characters who could make Del Boy seem about as sharp as a rubber duck. The only time I caught a real cold was when I bought 2,000 pairs of sunglasses at 20p a time and finally had to unload them at the same price after one of the wettest summers on record. I was a real 'Slippery Jim' and my smartest deal was completed with, of all companies, London Weekend Television. I got wind of the fact that they had struggled to shift a couple of hundred tracksuits and training shoes carrying the *World of Sport* logo. After I had made an initial inquiry about the gear, I was invited to the LWT headquarters at South Bank where a few months later Russell Harty interviewed me and where I was to be a so-called star of the *Saint and Greavsie* show. I was taken to a projection room by a couple of LWT sales people, and shown a special promotion film featuring the tracksuits. They gave me the big spiel about the quality of the gear that was all individually parcelled. 'Thank you very much, gents,' I said in my best Del Boy manner. 'I'm going to make you a take-it-or-leave-it offer.' They both looked like punters at a market stall, expecting to hear an offer of something like a tenner a throw. 'I'll give you a pound a parcel,' I said. 'That gear can only be knocked out in the markets and is so dated that no genuine sportswear chain will handle it.'

I was expecting to be shown the door, but they both shrugged their shoulders and we shook hands on the deal. They were just happy to get it off their shelves. Within a couple of days I had shifted all the parcels to market contacts at a fiver a throw. Del Boy would have been proud of me. It remains my nicest little earner out of LWT!

At the end of each business day I used to return to my one-room flat in Wanstead, passing most evenings by watching the box and sometimes nattering to the bloke in the adjoining flat. He was another Jimmy, and earned his daily bread as a professional punter. One day he was up, the next he was down but never once did he lose his cheerful optimism. 'I've got a great one for tomorrow,' he used to say. 'It's a cert.' But he was still in the flat when I returned to Irene and the kids, so I assumed not too many of his certs came in for him. I often wondered what happened to him, and was delighted to bump into him at Newmarket where I was watching the 1989 running of the 1000 Guineas. He looked a million dollars and told me, 'Things are going great, Jim, and I've got a cert for tomorrow!' It made me almost nostalgic for my Del Boy days, but, in all honesty, without Irene they were the emptiest times of my life.

When *The Sun* helped pick me off the floor I had no confidence that my sports page column would last and I joined Abbey Life Assurance Company as an insurance (pun intended) against not being wanted. Under the guidance of a good friend, Paul Revere, I settled into the world of insurance as comfortably as I had into the world of football. I am fascinated by anything to do with insurance, and I studied more fanatically than I had ever done in my school years. In no time at all I became an Associate at Abbey Life and was trusted with making presentations at major conferences. This was all a marvellous foundation for launching in later years my own insurance brokerage company that I run with Lynn, who learned the trade on the floor at Lloyds. I often stop and wonder what I might have achieved had I not lost more than five years to the bottle, but nobody can insure against that sort of thing happening. Even the most disciplined of people can get trapped by the demon drink. It creeps up on you when you are least expecting it, and suddenly you are in its deadly grip. But I managed to break the hold it had over me, and I hope that gives inspiration to anybody who may have the problem.

If Greavsie can beat the bottle, anybody can. Just take it one day at a time.

I was jogging along happily with my new life when I was approached by a flamboyant producer/director called Bernie Stringle, the genius behind the chimps' PG Tips commercials. I think Bernie must have seen a similarity between the chimps and me and decided that I was worth a programme. He asked me how much I wanted to be paid, and I said 'a monkey!' (Cockney slang for £500). We settled for peanuts, and Bernie and I got to work putting together a penetrating documentary called *Just for Today*, which was based on my book *This One's On Me*. The programme lasted 50 minutes, but I spent hours doing unscripted, direct-to-camera material which, unknowingly, was an apprenticeship for a new life that lay ahead.

One day in August 1980, Tony Flanagan – producer of ATV's *Star Soccer* – was casting around for a former footballer to work as an analyst on his Saturday night show that featured action highlights of matches involving teams based in the Midlands. The names of a procession of ex-players with Midlands connections were considered and discarded, and then Tony staggered his colleagues at an editorial meeting by saying, 'How about Greavsie?'

'Greavsie? But he's a piss-head.'

Tony tossed a copy of *The Sun* on to the desk. 'Well he's sober enough to produce an excellent column like this,' he said. 'He's obviously not frightened to speak his mind, and in that documentary *Just for Today* he proved he could work to camera like a real pro.'

There were mumblings about it being a bit stupid having a Cockney commenting on the Midlands football scene, but Jimmy Hill, Malcolm Allison and John Bond had made the London accent acceptable to all ears. And so the call went out, 'Get Greavsie.' *Star Soccer* Editor Trevor East and then the Sports Editor Gary Newbon contacted Norman Giller, who was my representative, to gauge my interest and my availability. Next my old England buddy Billy Wright came on in his ATV executive role to talk money.

My immediate reaction was: 'Birmingham? That's near the North Pole, ain't it?'

I was flattered to be approached, but I got the jitters just thinking about it.

I turned to the only person whose advice I really trusted. 'What shall I do, Irene?' I asked, honestly hoping she would dismiss the idea as stupid.

She did not mess about as she pointed me in a new direction in life. 'Jim,' she said, 'Get off your backside and up that M1!'

My television career was about to take off, and I was petrified. It was enough to drive a man to drink.

CHAPTER TWO

Of mice and men

First of all I wanted directions how to get to the ATV – soon to be Central – headquarters in Birmingham. 'You'll have no problems finding us, Jim,' said *Star Soccer* director Sydney (B. de Mille) Kilby. 'You spent some time in Milan so you'll quickly unravel the mysteries of Spaghetti Junction!' It was this sort of sense of humour that was to wrap itself around me and get me through a nervous start to my new life on the box.

I was one of those Cockneys for whom anything north of Watford was foreign land. Just the thought of going as far up the motorway as Birmingham to work threatened to give me a nosebleed. It was a mistaken attitude that kept me tied to London football clubs throughout my playing career, apart from an abortive and bruising three-month affair in Milan where I was homesick from the second I stepped off the plane (I was sozzled on arrival, as it happens, because it was in the days when I could only beat my fear of flying by boozing before and during the flight).

Over the next ten years, and thousands of miles, of constant commuting up and down the motorway I was to discover that I had made an error of a lifetime by dismissing the provinces as no-go areas. I have not met friendlier or more genuine people than those who became my new companions in Birmingham, and it made me realise what a wally I had been by cocking a deaf 'un to chances of playing for clubs in the Midlands.

In particular I regretted not taking the opportunity to join Brian Clough when he was manager at Derby County and I was coming to the end of my nine-year run at Tottenham. A message was passed to me on the football grapevine that Brian wanted to sign me. I fancied playing for Cloughie, but not for a Midlands club. Instead, I took the easy option and went down the road to West Ham where I lasted just one unsatisfactory season during which I lacked motivation and desire. They were the two vital sparks that I know Cloughie, the Great Motivator, would have given me. And I also now know that I would have had a great rapport with the Midlands fans.

Got it wrong again, Greavsie. You could have put another four or five years on your career by moving up to the Midlands, and the booze might not have become such a problem if you had kept playing at top level.

The first person I was introduced to by sports boss Gary Newbon on arriving at the ATV studios was the football reporter who would be working on the show with us. He was a young, fresh-faced journalist called Nick Owen, who had recently arrived in television after collecting a BA honours degree in classics at Leeds University (not a lot of people know that!). In the nearby newsroom a pretty presenter was preparing her script ready for the local round-up of news. She was Anne Diamond. The three of us had no idea that we were destined one day in the future to come together with an as yet unborn television company and in circumstances of high drama and, often, high farce.

Next on the tour of my new stamping ground I was reunited with executive sports chief Billy Wright, my first captain when I made my England debut during what seemed a lifetime ago. I played with Billy in the last three of his 105 international appearances for England in the days when he was the blond idol of football. He had skippered England across an incredible stretch of 90 matches, and had been the Black Country rock on which Wolves had built a legend of invincibility during their golden days of the 1950s. At the end of his distinguished playing career Billy had wrestled unhappily with management at Arsenal before going into television management, where you don't have to collect points every week to satisfy directors and spectators (perhaps if we did start awarding points for programmes we would possibly get a much-needed improvement in television management! I can certainly think of a few candidates for relegation).

Somebody unkindly reminded Billy that at the back end of his career I had got lucky and banged in five goals against him for Chelsea when Wolves were rated the mightiest club around. Dear old Billy then told this story against himself, 'I played hundreds of matches during my career, captained England and won 105 caps, skippered three championship-winning sides and lifted the FA Cup. But the only three things I seem to be remembered for are skippering the side beaten by the United States in the 1950 World Cup, being beaten all ends up when Puskas scored a magnificent goal in Hungary's 6–3 win at Wembley, and continually tackling Jimmy's shadow when he nipped in for five goals against Wolves in my last season as a player.'

'It's a funny old game, Bill,' I said.

Billy showed a few years later that he had not lost the iron will that made him such a great footballer and magnificent ambassador for the game and our country. He managed very quietly to beat the sort of booze problem that would have cut down lesser men. It was his greatest victory, and I know that his lovely wife – Joy of the Beverly Sisters – was delighted to get her old Billy back. I appeared on his *This is Your Life* tribute programme with the Saint, and while I made some tongue-in-cheek insulting remarks about him rather than the usual syrupy comments, I was full of admiration for the way he had got himself together and was once again the shining hero. Well done, Bill, old pal.

My first couple of appearances as football analyst on *Star Soccer* were worthy of a Monty Python sketch. If there was a wrong camera to look at, I looked at it. If there was a time when not to speak, I spoke. If there was some grammar what was to be mangled, I mangled it. I was in awe of the way Gary Newbon and Nick Owen read their Autocue scripts with a casual ease. It made me realise just how naïve I was about television. I had always been one of those viewers convinced that people looking out at me from the 20-inch screen were talking directly to me with a full grasp of what they were saying. I marvelled at how they were able to remember everything and talk with such authority while being watched by an audience of millions. But I quickly learned when I was on the other side of the camera that most of them are nodding and smiling at a screen that automatically reflects their words that have been carefully scripted before they go on air. Just thinking about the Autocue, and the possibility of being asked to use it, made me break into a sweat.

I need to back track here to explain my fear of the Autocue. When I left Kingswood secondary school at the age of fifteen to start my footballing apprenticeship with Chelsea in the spring of 1955 I went against the advice and wishes of my schoolteachers. I had just been made head boy of the school, and I was considered a good candidate for advanced education despite the fact that I was a tortoise when it came to reading. It used to take me twice as long as anybody else to plough through a text book, but I still managed to scramble through for good all-round results in my exams. Sport took my main concentration, and when I found out that I would be too old to gain Essex schools representative honours at cricket during the summer term I decided to accept the offer to join Chelsea and I left school at Easter.

My parents were delighted with my progress as a footballer, particularly as my lovely old Dad – a London tube train driver and a handy all-round sportsman in his time – was able to cop a hush-hush backhander of fifty quid in Irish notes in return for me agreeing to sign for Chelsea. Happy days! I had a brother and sister both bright enough to get teaching diplomas, but all I had to show for my schooling was a final report that I could read only slowly.

In those days nobody had ever heard of dyslexia. Dixie Dean, maybe. But dyslexia? It sounds like some sort of disease deserving of a Government health warning. It was Irene – who else? – who worked out that my problem was word blindness, and she has helped me and encouraged me to overcome it by slow, painstaking reading. But even now I can get words back to front when I try to read quickly. So that is why I was terrified of the Autocue. I am much happier making keyword notes for myself, jotting down one word or a short phrase that will bring to my mind an entire sentence. For instance, if I was facing the camera and had to spout that last sentence I would note down the words JOTTING NOTES. That would be enough to trigger the entire sentence. I would not recognise a split infinitive if you served it to me on a plate, but I do try to avoid clichés (like the plague). I know that I continue to occasionally murder the Queen's English, but – let's be honest – the royal brigade sometimes trample on Greavsie's English with their hizes instead of houses, lynges instead of lounges and pynds instead of pounds. Okay, yah?

Gary Newbon protected me like a mother hen, and I have him to thank for steering me through my early appearances on *Star Soccer* and the Friday evening preview programmes. I was convinced I was going to be politely asked to leave after my first few weeks, and I kept open my options to stay in the insurance business.

The big mistake I made in my first couple of shows was trying to ape the likes of Jimmy Hill and Malcolm Allison, discussing tactics and technique. What I was trying to say went over my head, let alone that of any viewer. Anybody who knew me in my playing days will tell you that I am to tactics what Edwina Currie is to egg production. I have always talked about the game in simplistic terms. It's a simple game, and is complicated only by coaches who disappear up their rear end with mumbo jumbo talk that baffles players and leads to so much of the dull, sterile play that we witness today.

In my third appearance, by which time I had started to conquer my nerves, I was relaxed enough to talk about the game exactly as I would if I was standing on the terraces. There was an obvious off-side goal that was allowed to stand, and I said: 'Blimey, if I'd scored that one I would have kissed the ref. And if I'd been in the opposing team I would have told the linesman where to stick his flag.'

It just came out naturally, and Gary Newbon laughed out loud and the technicians on the studio floor were also falling about laughing.

Blimey, Greavsie, You're on to something here. Just be yourself, my son. Leave the tactical stuff to Jimmy Hill. Let him *disappear with a flash and a bang.*

From that moment on my television career was up and running, and I found out just what a powerful medium it is. I could not walk anywhere in the Midlands without being mobbed by people wanting to pump my hand. I had known nothing like it, even when I was knocking goals in at the peak of my playing days. I don't say this in praise of myself, but just to illustrate the reaction you get when you become a regular on the small screen. I was determined not to become affected by the sudden adulation that dwarfed anything I had known as a player, but there are plenty of people in television who will tell you that it went to my head (more of that later).

Even the press were nice to me: 'Jimmy Greaves has brought something almost unheard of to football punditry – a sense of humour,' said the *Sunday Times*. 'Greavsie is the cheeky chappie of TV sport who has brought a rare and much-needed smile to the sad face of soccer,' said *The Sun*. 'He is irreverent, savagely honest, often hilarious and sometimes bordering on the irresponsible, which makes his act compulsive viewing and certainly more entertaining than the football that he is analysing,' said the *Mail*.

I never used to read reports of the matches in which I played, but I did read the television critics – not because I was seeking praise, but so that I could learn from any constructive criticism about a world that was foreign to me. There was the occasional kick in the shins ('Jimmy Greaves sounds as if he has taken elocution lessons from Alf Garnett'), but on the whole I came out of it unscathed and I was encouraged to step up my sort of 'voice of the people' approach to football. Looking back at video tape recordings of my early appearances, my face appeared as miserable as an untidy grave, and I was glad of the advice of Central fishing expert Terry Thomas, who told me: 'Loosen up and smile, Jimmy. You've got a smile that lights up the screen. People don't want to switch on and see you looking like an undertaker.'

So I started smiling along with the wisecracks, which prompted one sports page critic, who thought I was treating football with less reverence than it deserved, to write: 'Why doesn't Greaves go the whole way and put on a clown's suit? He was one of the all-time great footballers, but now all he can do is poke fun at the game to which he owes so much.'

This particular writer, who reported many of my matches, obviously did not get to know me. Even during my playing days I used to send up the game and the people in it who I thought were taking it too seriously. My casual attitude used to drive theorists like Walter Winterbottom, Alf Ramsey, Bill Nicholson and Ron Greenwood up the wall. I will always maintain that football should be fun, and if the coaches who have got a stranglehold on the game would only loosen up and let the players express themselves as entertainers our soccer – both at international and domestic level – would be all the better for it (ends boring football lecture).

Once I had the reputation for being funny my job became tougher, and I was conscious of *trying* to be funny instead of letting any wisecracks come naturally. But in those early days on *Star Soccer* I thoroughly enjoyed myself. I quickly settled into a routine at what became Central Television, and felt as comfortable as in my footballing days. It was just like being back with a winning team, and I looked forward to going into the office where there was the sort of dressing room type of camaraderie I had known as a player. Gary Newbon became my good friend, and I became his trusted confidant even though I used him unmercifully for the butt of many of my jokes. Once while on air I held up a book that I was going to present to him. It was called *The Fat Pig's Story*. Within a couple of years we were calling each other much worse than that, and meaning it.

I had not lost my thirst for drink, and I became known as 'The Tea Boy' at Central because I planted myself by the tea-making machine and got through at least 20 cups a day. I told Gary that I preferred coffee, and he thoughtfully had a coffee machine installed in the office for me. Sadly, there would come the day when he would have willingly made it an arsenic machine.

'Make us a cup, Greavsie,' became a familiar cry at Central as everybody – from executives, presenters, secretaries and crew – used to queue waiting for me to provide them with tea or coffee. It also became part of my routine to go out every Saturday evening to the Cheung Yin restaurant to get a massive takeaway order for the team working on the late-night *Star Soccer* show. This went on for months until we got a written complaint from the head of security saying that leaving the remains of our Chinese food in the office had led to an invasion of mice. We were ordered to stop bringing the food into the office. I sent a spoof reply back to the security chief that read, 'We shall be reporting you to the European commission for mice rights. By banning the Chinese takeaway binge you are depriving our children of nourishment. Be nice to the mice!' I signed it Mickey and Minnie Mouse.

I was not popular with everybody at Central. I arrived one Friday evening for the preview show and after parking my car went to pat the head of the car park attendant's dog which responded by biting me. From then on I called it Norman Hunter.

Around about that time I also had an odd experience with a camel called Stirling. Ladbrokes arranged a charity camel race at Crayford, and it was a sign of my growing 'celebrity' status that I was invited to ride one of the entrants. I won't make you cringe with hump jokes, but suffice to say that I won the race by a short head from Grand National hero Bob Champion, who rode his camel as if it was Aldaniti. All I did was cling on for dear life and pray to Allah. Press photographers clamoured for a picture of me with the camel after the race, and I started kissing it as they clicked away. Then the camel owner said without a flicker of a smile. 'Careful, Jim. You can get syphilis if a camel bites you.' I replied with something to the effect that if the bloody camel bit me I would bite back and give him alcohol poisoning. But the warning sank in, and I gave Stirling plenty of room. Can you imagine going home to your missus and saying that you had caught syphilis from a camel? The mind boggles.

One other incident from around that time always makes me smile when I think of it. Cricket fanatics Frank Nicklin and Reg Hayter invited me to play for their Fleet Street Strollers team in a friendly in Frank's home county of Derbyshire. I was torn between choosing football or cricket for my career when I was leaving school, and fancied myself as the new Godfrey Evans of wicket-keepers. I had not played for several years, but answered the call with some enthusiasm. It meant a round trip of around 300 miles from the new bungalow home in Little Baddow, near Chelmsford in Essex, where Irene and I had dropped anchor after escaping our bad memories of our old manor at Upminster. I was on the road for eight hours and in between managed to get myself bowled first ball. What made it so amusing was that the following week the local Derbyshire paper was sent to me. It featured a seven column back page headline – as big as anything I had received as a footballer – and it screamed, GREAVES FLOPS WITH A DUCK. The price of fame!

My first season with the *Star Soccer* team went so well that I was given a larger canvas, and I started to contribute a regular feature called The Greaves Report, in which I took an off-beat look at sport. I played tennis with my fellow left hander John McEnroe (who was a real charmer and nothing like his super-brat image), faced Bob Willis bowling flat out (I actually managed to see a couple of the balls), wrestled with Kendo Nagasaki (and found out a whole new meaning to horizontal hold), played bowls, croquet, tried arm wrestling (but quickly gave it the elbow), went fishing, motor cycled with Barry Sheene, actually got Sebastian Coe to stand still for a chat, hit double tops with Eric Bristow and played squash with Jonah Barrington. I also gave the first out-of-the-ring television exposure to an up-and-coming young heavyweight called Frank Bruno. I drove him up to Birmingham in a powerful Mercedes owned by his manager Terry Lawless. On the way I explained to Frank that I wanted him to put the gloves on and spar with me in a local gymnasium while I interviewed him.

The sparring session would have made a great sketch for a comedy show. Frank is six inches taller than me, and I was having trouble getting past his long arms to ask my questions. In those early days in his career muscular Frank was weighing about 15 stone, and I had ballooned up from my playing days weight of 10 stone 7 pounds to around 13 stone. I was a welterweight masquerading in an out-of-condition heavyweight's body. Director Syd Kilby's plan was that I should 'fight' my way inside Frank's reach and put a question each time I got to close quarters. Syd didn't realise the effort and energy you use just when sparring, particularly against a giant like Bruno. Each time I fought my way close enough to ask a question I was breathing like a wounded bull.

I would start the interview and then the soundman would interrupt and say, 'All I can hear is Greavsie's heavy breathing.'

'You could sell the soundtrack for a bleedin' blue movie,' I said between gasps for air.

After about six tries, it was left to Jim to fix it. I told Syd Kilby to forget about the sparring, and I said to Bruno: 'I'll tell you what, Frank, you rest against the ropes in the corner and I'll interview you there.'

A pity the cameras didn't follow us back down the motorway when we left Birmingham. We stopped off at a service station for a bite to eat and we had the place in uproar. I kept going up to the biggest, toughest lorry drivers I could find and challenging them to a fight. Then I'd point at Frank and say: 'I think you should know that I'll be bringing on a sub.'

The biggest laugh of the day was on me. Frank filled three trays with food, and I was left to pay the bill.

We had a return match a year later, and that was even funnier although my eyes water at the memory. By then I was doing a regular enjoyable stint on the *Saturday Show*, a kids' programme presented by Tommy Boyd and Isla St Clair. I had learned from our first meeting in front of the cameras, and this time I rehearsed the interview with Frank before our 'live' sparring session. I worked it out with him that I would ask a question and then lightly hit him with three pulled punches. Bang, bang, bang.

Then Frank would reply and hit me with three light punches. Bang, bang, bang.

We got a nice rhythm going at rehearsal. Question – bang, bang, bang. Answer – bang, bang, bang.

Then we went 'live' with the interview in the middle of a ring in the studio – and Frank suddenly froze with the sort of camera fright that many, me included, had experienced before him.

I asked my first question and lightly hit Frank with three punches. He replied and lightly landed his three punches. I asked my second question and he replied, and we gradually got into the rhythm. By the time of my fifth question Frank began to relax, but somehow managed to get out of synchronisation.

I asked my question – bang, bang, bang. Instead of replying as we had agreed Frank landed three punches that were twice as hard as usual and caught me completely unawares. My knees buckled and I fell forward into Frank's arms with my head spinning and water streaming from my eyes.

The studio crew were all folded up laughing off camera as I somehow managed to get through the interview. I got myself locked into a close-quarter clinch rather than risk taking any more out-of-time punches.

My most frightening experience came when I tried my hand at hang gliding. Somehow, along with beating the bottle, I also conquered my fear of flying (well, almost). I must have done because I agreed to go up in a two-man hang glider with professional pilot Rory McCarthy. He is an incredible character, a real action man who is only happy when he is sailing across the sky like a bird. He was once rescued from the summit of Mt Blanc when he got trapped while trying to fly from the highest point in Europe, but I knew I was in safe company because he is rated one of the world's great hang gliding experts.

It was early in December and a strong, icy wind was blowing as we took off from Dunstable Downs in Bedfordshire. We had been up for about ten minutes soaring at 300 feet above the Downs like Siamese eagles when the glider was caught by a sudden 60 mph gust. It swept us towards the 1000 feet mark, and Rory deliberately stalled the glider to stop us being blown towards a built-up area. We came out of the sky as if we had been hit by anti-aircraft fire, with Rory working like a

Superman to control our drop. I just spread myself out and tried to remember whether I'd had the good sense to top up my insurance. We came down in light bracken that broke our fall, and we were lucky enough to land on top of the smashed glider. Both Rory and I were shaken and bruised, but escaped without injury.

Producer Jeff 'What are the odds?' Farmer checked that we were all right, and then said with his typical humour: 'You never were any good in the air, Greavsie.'

The fact that being a witness to the accident had turned Jeff as white as a sheet showed just how close Rory and I had come to a fatal crash.

As soon as I got home I increased my insurance.

My first breakthrough on to network television came during the 1982 World Cup finals when I was invited to be a member of the ITV panel under the chairmanship of Brian Moore. It meant a return to the London Weekend Television studios where I had made my nervous appearance on the Russell Harty show three years earlier. And once again my first port of call was the loo where I threw up before going on air. This time it was not booze, nor was it nerves. I was suffering from food poisoning, but I kept it quiet because I did not want to miss the chance of joining in one of television's big sporting jamborees.

The World Cup panels had first been introduced during the 1970 finals when the likes of Malcolm Allison, Derek Dougan, Pat Crerand and Bob McNab became household names by mouthing off about the lads sweating it out on the pitches in the heat and thin air of Mexico. I detested their pontificating, and thought they made right wallies of themselves. Now here I was becoming one of them.

What a two-faced git you've become, Greavsie. You were an outspoken critic of the panellists because you didn't think it fair that they should take cheap pot shots at players from the comfort of the studio. Now you are on the same band wagon. You've sold your soul, my son, just to get your face on the small screen. Still, if I don't do it somebody else will and, of course, I've got some original views to contribute. Conceited sod.

I had joined a new breed of broadcasters. I was not a commentator, but an 'opinionator' (there's a new word worthy of the attention of lexicographers).

'What d'you do for a living, Dad?'
'I'm an opinionator, son.'
'What's an opinionator?'
'It's somebody who has power without responsibility, and the ability to spout off on any subject without worrying too much about the consequences of what comes out of the mouth. All you need is an opinion and the opportunity to voice it. Television is full of professional opinionators, and I've become one of the noisiest of them.'

So I took my opinions on to the ITV panel under the conscientious control of Brian Moore, one of the best pros in the business and as contrasting to me as it is possible to be. Mooro is sober, refined, articulate, organised, well-informed, in total control of his thoughts and deeds – an out-and-out perfectionist who is a credit to his profession. We have a mutual respect for each other even though I sometimes manage to get up Brian's nose with my casual, laid-back attitude. As chairman of the World Cup panel he was in charge of a posse of outspoken football rebels including George Best, Jack Charlton, Mike Channon, Denis Law, Ian St John and, the big daddy of the pundits, Brian Clough. Somehow Mooro kept us under some sort of control as we attempted to turn the World Cup into a foot-and-mouth tournament.

It was like a game of musical chairs in the studio, with panellists queueing for places on the set to condemn, crucify, compliment and, occasionally, cheer the players and managers struggling for success in Spain. It was easy to play a blinder in the studio. I managed to pick eventual winners Italy from the first day as the likely champions, and could have eaten free meals for life in England's multitude of Italian restaurants where every waiter and every chef is a soccer nut.

The craziest thing of all was having George Best sitting in the studio in London watching his former Irish international team-mates progressing to the quarter finals. They would have done even better had they had the sense to select George, who was looking trim and fit following two seasons in the USA. Bestie is the greatest footballer of my lifetime, and I include the likes of Pele, Di Stefano, Puskas, Eusebio, Maradona, Cruyff, Matthews and Finney in that assessment. Even if he had been half fit, he would have been worth his place in the Irish squad and it was beyond my comprehension that they ignored him.

I had a lot of time to talk to George, who is one of the nicest blokes you could wish to meet. Like me, he has had problems with booze and has occasionally fallen back into the arms of the bottle. We agreed that the then Tottenham star Glenn Hoddle and United skipper Bryan Robson were the only modern-day English footballers who would rate in the class of the great players of our era, and we were both of the opinion that all coaches should be locked in a huge stadium where they could bore each other to death with their tactical theories. The biggest change in the game since finishing our League careers was, we decided, the emergence of 'personality' managers. They had become bigger than the game and were better known than the players, which we agreed was a bad thing for football.

The biggest of the personalities, of course, was on the World Cup panel with us – Cloughie – but both George and I were of the opinion that his saving grace was that he could really manage and was able to put action where his mouth is. Cloughie was subdued with his views in comparison with previous television appearances, but was still the man viewers switched on to see and hear.

I was given the last word on the 1982 World Cup, and almost gave Mooro a heart attack when I said: 'These finals have all been about long balls, short balls, square balls, through balls, high balls, low balls, and to you, Brian, I would just like to say ... (a deliberate pause) ... it's been a pleasure being here on the panel.'

My stock shot up after my World Cup appearances, and I was lucky enough to get a good press nationwide. My performances came as a surprise to most people who did not realise I had been serving an apprenticeship in the television game with Central. I knew I must have made an impact because suddenly the demand for interviews and personal appearances quadrupled. I had also made my mark with the chiefs of ITV Sport and I was rewarded with a regular spot on *World of Sport*, linking up 'live' with Ian St John in *On the Ball* from my base in Birmingham. This laid the foundation for what was to become the *Saint and Greavsie Show*.

And while this was all going on the forces of fate were working to bring Anne Diamond, Nick Owen and me together in the unlikely setting of Camden Lock. We were about to have indigestion for breakfast.

CHAPTER THREE

Carry on TV-am

If a scriptwriter were to put down on paper the off-camera events and shenanigans at TV-am since the company's birth he would have a soap opera to match *Dallas* or *Dynasty*, a farce suitable for the *Carry On* series, great drama of Shakespearian proportions, and, finally, a story of an incredible triumph against all the odds. TV-am or not TV-am: that was the question when I arrived in May 1983 just ahead of the London Electricity Board representative, who gave the ultimatum that if the electricity bill was not paid within half an hour he would cut off the supply to the studios. TV-am came *that* close to a total black-out.

I got a ringside seat for the greatest TV show on earth thanks (or no thanks) to my pal Norman Giller, who told new Editor-in-Chief Greg Dyke that I was the ideal man to present a hard-hitting sports opinion column of the air. Greg, newly arrived from LWT with the simple brief to save TV-am from the knackers yard in the wake of the 'Famous Five', called me in for a chat. My first reaction when I saw 'Egg Cup Towers' nestling on the banks of Camden Lock in the Arsenal territory of North London was that the person who planned it must have been in a fog at the time. Faulty Towers more like it. I wondered if it was the same bloke who provided the knitting pattern for Spaghetti Junction. I was then introduced to Greg Dyke, the man with his finger in the gushing hole in the TV-am dyke. He was bearded and balding and his casual jeans and tee-shirt attire were not exactly what you would call executive style.

'What do you know about television?' was Greg's opening shot.

'Enough to know which camera to look at when the red light comes on,' I said.

'No, not the camera side of television,' said Greg, tugging impatiently at his beard. 'I mean the important side that the punters watch. Do you *watch* the box?'

'I've become a screencholic since giving up the booze,' I said truthfully. 'I watch it until the little dot disappears after the epilogue. I even watch *Good Morning Britain*!'

'Just what I wanted to hear,' said Greg, his eyes bulging with enthusiasm. 'You can be our television previewer. It will be a five minute spot and I want you to tell viewers what they should and shouldn't watch. All I ask of you is that you do it with a bit of humour. No over-the-head highbrow stuff. We're looking to go down market.'

'That's very flattering of you,' I chuckled. 'You can't get much more down market than me.'

'No offence, Jim,' said Greg, who had so much energy pouring out of him that they could have plugged him into the mains and not had to worry about an electricity bill. 'I want us to become *The Sun* of the air, not the toffee-nosed *Telegraph* like the other lot made it.'

At this point Michael Parkinson, one of the survivors of 'the other lot,' walked into the office. He and his wife Mary were holding the fort on air before going off to Australia for a summer break. 'Jimmy's joining us,' said Greg.

'Marvellous,' said Parky. 'Our sports coverage could do with some beefing up.'

'He's going to be our television previewer,' said Greg.

'Oh, I see,' said Parky, his eyes clouding over. 'That's, uh, very interesting.' Greavsie becoming the television previewer for *Good Morning Britain* must have made as much sense to him as Freddie Trueman reading the news. As one of the founders of TV-am he had been under enormous pressure in the previous few weeks and looked shell-shocked and in need of that trip Down Under.

Parky had been a leading member of the ambitious TV-am consortium which was awarded the lucrative breakfast television franchise by the Independent Broadcasting Authority in December 1980. Peter Jay was the chairman and chief executive, and in the star-studded team with Parky were David Frost, Anna Ford, Angela Rippon, Robert Kee and Esther Rantzen, who later dropped out to have a baby, leaving behind the 'Famous Five'. Over the following months quite a few of the others must have felt they were having babies!

For a start, there was a gigantic cock-up on the contracts front. The hilarious story I've been told is that when the individual contracts were sent out to the 'Famous Five' they were put into the wrong envelopes. You can imagine the explosive reactions when, purely by chance, Robert Kee found he was being paid less than Anna Ford, and Angela Rippon apparently discovered that her pay was paltry compared with the others. So before they even reached the airways there was dissent in the camp.

I switched on for the launching of TV-am on the morning of February 1, 1983. There was the magnificent aerial shot of hundreds of people forming the *Good Morning Britain* opening title (so good that it survived all of TV-am's revolutions) and then there was the familiar face of Frostie. 'Hello, good morning and welcome,' he said. It was a nice, warm, friendly start. And from there on it was downhill all the way. Items were being presented as if they were carved in stone and brought down from Mount Sinai. It was all too heavy and formal and I, along with thousands of others, quickly switched over to the BBC where Frank Bough and Selina Scott had been comfortably established for three weeks with their *Breakfast Time* show.

Within a month the 'Famous Five' had an audience that had dwindled to 300,000 and by the middle of March they had so few viewers that the programme was officially zero-rated. BBC's figures had gone up to 1.6 million, and among the scores of jokes buzzing around was that TV-am were going to change the name of their programme from *Good Morning Britain* to *Is There Anybody Out There?*

It was no laughing matter for the 'Famous Five' and with advertisers reluctant to spend any money there was suddenly a serious financial crisis looming. Peter Jay resigned and was replaced as temporary Chief Executive by Jonathan Aitken MP.

In April 1983 Angela Rippon and Anna Ford departed in such a blaze of publicity that it's a wonder Egg Cup Towers didn't burn down. Angry Anna Ford faced rival cameras and said: 'There's been a great deal of treachery going on behind our backs.' She then got some sort of satisfaction by throwing a glass of white wine in Jonathan Aitken's face during a private party. All that was missing was JR and his stetson and the well-oiled Sue-Ellen.

Greg Dyke, described as a '37-year-old whizz kid,' took over as Editor-in-Chief and I was among his first signings along with keep-fit expert 'Mad' Lizzie Webb and weather wise Wincey Willis. My old Birmingham side-kick Nick Owen, who had joined the original TV-am team as a sports presenter, was about to be promoted to full-time couch duty while Parky was in Australia, with Henry Kelly joining as a co-presenter. The enthusiastic Mike Morris would step into Nick's sports shoes, with a young sports reporter called Richard Keys coming in as his deputy.

Dykie then made his two most inspired signings. 'You worked at Central when Anne Diamond was there, didn't you,' he said to me one day. 'What d'you think of her?'

'Very pretty, very professional,' I said. 'One of the best presenters I've seen.'

By then Anne had joined the BBC in London, and a week later Dykie announced that he had signed her for the TV-am team. 'I didn't want to come,' she said later. 'I was very content at the BBC and at that time TV-am was a laughing stock. But Greg called me a coward and said I was frightened of what was the last great television challenge. It was the force of his personality and his sheer enthusiasm that persuaded me to give it a go.'

I was less impressed when Dykie announced that he had also signed a small felt puppet answering to the name of Roland Rat. Dave Claridge, who had a big hand in the 'orrible rodent's rise from the gutter, brought Roland to TV-am to entertain the younger viewers.

Thanks largely to Greg Dyke's policy of concentrating on 'popular' television, TV-am started to close the gap on BBC's *Breakfast Time* and in less than a year we had overhauled them in the ratings. But our self congratulations were rather muted because everybody was giving the credit to Roland bloody Rat for increasing our share of the audience. One rival across at the Beeb said, 'It's the first time a rat has come to the aid of a sinking ship.'

I preferred to think the improvement in ratings was due to the excellent presenting standards being set by Anne Diamond and Nick Owen. They had a good made-in-Brum chemistry between them, and their interviewing technique made guests on the sofa relax and come up with fascinating answers to questions that were probing without being prying. Dykie further beefed up the content by bringing in king of the gossip columnists Nigel Dempster, pop and film specialist Paul Gambaccini and agony aunt Claire 'Luvvie' Rayner. Jayne 'Legs' Irving brought sparkle to the *After Nine* spot aimed at housewives, and 'Mad Lizzie' had the nation hopping about in a high-kicking search for fitness. I was only a part-time contributor, but there was such a strong team spirit that I felt a total commitment to what had become a fight for survival. My job on the sofa was made much easier by the back-up work of respected showbusiness journalist Joe Steeples, who did all the research for me and selected the clips of programmes that I was previewing. In January 1984 our news output was given a boost by the arrival of that master of newsreaders, Gordon Honeycombe.

There was sadness stirred in with the success that we were having as the programmes pulled in more and more viewers. Two legendary ladies of the small screen, Diana Dors and Pat Phoenix, joined the TV-am team for what were tragically short stays.

Diana used to come to the studio with her husband, actor Alan Lake, in tow. Alan had been fighting 'The Problem' for a long time, and he and I had several quiet chats about our experiences and he admitted that he was still having a tough job beating the depressions that drop from out of nowhere on recovering alcoholics. He was a talented actor in his own right, and it was sad to see him brooding in the background while Diana took the spotlight. 'My lady is fantastic, isn't she,' he said. 'You wouldn't believe she has been battling against a serious illness. Thank God she's beaten it. I don't know what I'd do without her.'

Poor Diana was dead from cancer within a couple of months. Alan couldn't cope with the loss, and put a gun to his head. It's a sad old life.

I also talked off set about 'The Problem' to actor Tony Booth, who had played the Scouse son-in-law of Alf Garnett. He had been encouraged to pull himself together by Pat Phoenix, the actress who will always be lovingly remembered for her stunning performances as Elsie Tanner in *Coronation Street*. Tony used to accompany Pat to the TV-am studio for her appearances before she, too, was taken from us by cancer. My heart went out to Tony, who married Pat on her death bed. It was chilling how Diana and Pat had been so closely linked by fate in the final acts of their lives. Both were gorgeous ladies who made a big impact on TV-am during what were, regrettably, brief but memorable contributions.

★ ★ ★

As well as *Good Morning Britain* was doing in the ratings war with BBC's *Breakfast Time,* TV-am was losing money in a spectacular and worrying way. It was pouring away like blood out of a gaping wound. I was having to wait weeks, sometimes months, for my fees and full-time staff members had to agree to take 'voluntary' pay cuts. Losses had spiralled to £12 million a year, and Camden Lock was running deep with rumours that the station was only weeks, perhaps days, from being closed down.

Timothy Aitken took over from his cousin, Jonathan, as chairman of the ailing company, and Greg Dyke moved on to new pastures after just over a year of miracle working. Most of his ideas were winners, and the only time he was threatened with a staff mutiny was when he had the presenters reading out the bingo numbers from the newspapers. They will tell you that it was the lowest spot in their television careers.

Greg could point with understandable pride to the fact that by the time he quit he had built up the audience from 200,000 to nearly 1,500,000. This was the foundation on which the company was to build its success out of the wreckage of near-disaster. Greg later became the boss of London Weekend Television where he had first made a major impact as producer of the innovative *Six O'clock Show.* It was Greg who master-minded the ITV takeover of League football, putting together the idea for the imaginative package of 'live' matches. Even now, I bet he misses our regular games of indoor football with a Sellotaped paper ball in the TV-am corridors. We miss his Matthews-style runs (Jessie Matthews, that is), and his kisses and cuddles whenever he scored. Fortunately it was not very often.

A new force in the slim, immaculately groomed shape of Bruce Gyngell was about to blow like a hurricane through the TV-am corridors of power. If he wanted to play with the ball, we would have to change to Aussie-rules football.

The amazing 'Pink Panther' of the antipodes was about to pounce, and TV-am would never be the same again.

If there is a more enterprising, energetic and eccentric man in the world of television than Bruce Gyngell then I have not come across him. From the second he waltzed like a fire-breathing Matilda into Egg Cup Towers, he was what is known in modern jargon as a 'hands on' manager. He came in as managing director, but soon had his hands on every control button in the building and this triggered a 'hands off' reaction from Greg Dyke, who made his exit shortly after Gyngell's arrival. Greg was soon followed by director of programmes Mike Hollingsworth, whose power struggle with Gyngell made the egg cups rattle on the roof of the TV-am building.

It was Mike who finished up on toast (a sort of ego on toast), and he was soon on his bike to more challenging fields. Just to complicate matters, Mike and Anne Diamond had started a raging romance that has since been blessed with two well-publicised babies. At one stage it got to the point where the gossip columns were heaving with stories that Gyngell had ordered Anne to marry the father of her children or quit. But I knew that old Brucie would be too canny a character to lose his trump Diamond, the queen of the TV-am pack. It was all much more dramatic and spellbinding than any television soap opera.

I doubt if any managing director in the history of British television has made such an immediate impact as Gyngell. He went on bombing raids in every department in an almost maniacal search for new efficiency and economies. Only he knew the real seriousness of the situation, and the stark reality was that TV-am was a bank manager's nod from closure. He pruned the staff from 483 to 341 within eight months, never openly sacking anybody but using his persuasive powers to convince departing staff members that they were doing the noble thing by leaving.

Bold Bruce took over all money matters and proved himself a real 'Goldfinger' Gyngell when it came to financial juggling. The company had accumulated losses of more than £15 million when he arrived on his mercy dash from Australia, and he had to beg advance money from advertisers to pay the staff wages. He insisted on signing every cheque and authorising every purchase, and within two years of first prudent and then bold house-keeping he was able to show company profits running into millions. I looked on from my ringside seat wearing my insurance salesman's hat and thought to myself, 'Blimey, I wonder what he'd be like at selling insurance?'

Gyngell was poking his nose into so many people's jobs that I fully expected to walk into the studio one day and find him presenting the programme. And he could have done it, too. The grandson of a ship's carpenter who settled Down Under, he began his television career as an anchorman in the United States on NBC's highly regarded *Today* show in the 1950s. With this experience under his belt he returned home in 1956 to enjoy the distinction of being the first person to appear on television in Australia. He then had wide involvement in management that shaped him for what looked the impossible task of saving TV-am.

His intense and sincere interest in Buddhism and his leanings towards Eastern mysticism, macrobiotic diets and meditation help make him one of the most unforgettable characters ever to have crossed my path. There was criticism of his deep involvement with Insight, the Californian consciousness-raising cult that was popularised in Britain by Arianna Stassinopoulos. But those TV-am employees whom Bruce introduced to the self-awareness movement swear that it has improved their quality of life and their self belief, and they are unswerving 'Gyngell Disciples.'

Mind you, there have been moments when we have wondered if the pressure was sending Bruce off his rocker. We have called him the 'Pink Panther' since the day he issued a directive that every presenter appearing on the programme should wear bright clothing, preferably pink. 'I want you to convey warmth and happiness to our viewers,' he instructed. 'It helps brighten up people's lives and removes the misery. Pink has a healing quality about it. We must make our programme seem as bright and as warming as an eternal summer.'

Bruce could not understand it when the majority of his staff were less than enthusiastic when he tried to get them to sing a TV-am company song before the start of each editorial meeting, and he also met some opposition when he suggested all his presenters should have regular sunbed treatment. 'I'm sick of the sight of pasty-faced Poms,' he said.

I thought it was hilarious, but there were some dark looks about the place.

Gyngell upset fellow directors on the Camden board when he reacted to IBA criticism of TV-am's editorial output by staging a private West End vaudeville review. He lampooned the IBA report by dressing up in the role of a naughty schoolboy being punished on stage by a headmaster portrayed by actor John Wells. But while he was apparently treating the IBA criticisms as a joke, he took note of all that was said and stengthened the TV-am editorial news and religious output.

Very quietly, he had not only turned the sinking ship away from the rocks but now had it back on its original 'explain and entertain' course.

Love him or loathe him, I am convinced that TV-am would have gone out of business but for the expertise and enthusiasm that Gyngell brought to his rescue mission. Amazingly, he managed to find time to fall in love with features editor Kathy Rowan, marrying her shortly before the arrival of their son Adam. See what I mean about a soap opera?

A year or so later the job nearly killed him.

Roland Rat jumped overboard in 1985 and swam across the channel to the BBC. We missed the little rat, but this allowed the potty but talented Timothy Mallett the chance to establish *Wacaday* as the most popular kid's programme on television. The rat may have abandoned the Camden Lock ship, but TV-am survived and the viewing figures started to leap above the 2 million mark.

There were some marvellous and memorable moments that helped build and then hold the TV-am audience. Nick Owen gave the station a prestigious boost with what he thought was an exclusive interview with Princess Michael of Kent in the wake of sensational allegations of her father's alleged involvement with Hitler's SS. BBC sunk to unheard of depths by pirating the interview, and the following publicity helped increase the stature of TV-am. From the sublime to the ridiculous, Nick then got into the headlines by having his trousers tugged off him by couch celebrity Pamela Stephenson (what on earth do they put in the water in Aussieland?). I was in the studio that morning and quickly realised that Nick had not found the incident as amusing as he was pretending for the cameras. In trying to escape Pamela's mad attentions he had aggravated an old back injury and was in agony for weeks afterwards.

If you believe all you read about Anne Diamond you will get the impression she is cold and aloof from her colleagues, and full of airs and graces. She is certainly a perfectionist who does not suffer fools gladly, but off camera I have always found her pleasant and thoughtful. She struggles to forgive me some of my grammatical cock-ups (I feel her wince when I fall into the old Cockney trap of saying 'I done' instead of 'I did') but I respect her for being one of the finest interviewers on television.

She knows how to put the right question at the right time and then, just as important, how to shut up and listen.

Anne – Lady Anne, as I dubbed her – knows she is superior at her job, and makes sure she gets the best possible deal for her talent which possibly leads to some off-screen jealousy. Good luck to her, I say. Something I have discovered in my short television life is that the programme makers will trample all over you and get you on the cheap if you let them. Anne knows how to stand up for herself, and she proved it in an electric interview with old Labour warhorse Denis Healey who was sitting on the sofa in the summer of 1987 alongside former Tory Defence Secretary Michael Heseltine. TV-am viewers saw just the start of the drama when Anne questioned Healey on newspaper stories about his wife Edna having paid to have a hip operation rather than going on the NHS.

Healey's florid face went purple, and he accused TV-am of 'a classical dirty trick' by inviting him to speak about the Venice economic summit when they really wanted to quiz him about his wife. He then went OTT by asking Anne, who was plainly pregnant, where she planned to have her baby. She stood her ground, and rightly protested that she was a journalist not a politician and that she was merely asking questions about the day's news.

During the commercial break, Healey brought gasps of astonishment from everybody in earshot when he ripped into Anne with a volley of abuse.

He then tried to storm off set, forgetting that he was still connected to his neck microphone cable that was wound round the leg of the sofa. If was like a scene from a Frank Spencer comedy as he struggled to extricate himself.

Political editor Adam Boulton was just off camera, and as Healey went past him in a rage he poked him heavily in the chest and made some less than complimentary remarks about TV-am.

Michael Heseltine took great delight in confirming all that had happened to a posse of newspaper reporters, scoring political points in the build-up to the general election. And, of course, every headline was marvellous publicity for TV-am.

I rated Anne Diamond and Nick Owen the best double act in the world of television interviewing, and I thought it was a bad career move by Nick when he succumbed to an approach by Thames Sport to become 'the head and shoulders' of ITV

Sport, with *Midweek Sports Special* as his main platform. It's the view of this opinionator that he allowed the sports fan inside him to over-rule his common sense. His new job presented him with little chance to do anything but introductory work instead of the celebrity interviewing at which he was becoming such a master. He also lost the army of women admirers he had built up during his successful stint on the TV-am couch. Jayne Irving was another sad loss when she quit TV-am for BBC's *Open Air* programme. I reckon an Owen–Irving partnership would have been a winning combination for the Camden Lock couch.

Adrian Brown, an outstanding young reporter, was taken off the road to replace Nick, and it proved a disastrous appointment. Adrian, such a master when out on location covering the big news stories, felt like a prisoner on the sofa. It was painful to watch him struggling to get his mind and mouth into working order, and Anne had to keep coming to his rescue during 'live' interviews in the studio. After four months of agony Adrian was big enough to ask if he could go back on the road.

Mike Morris and Richard Keys took turns to share the couch with Anne until Mike emerged as the number one choice of generalissimo Gyngell. Mike has had to take more than his fair share of stick from the critics. I reckon he does a difficult job well, and with Lorraine Kelly, is gradually restoring the magic that was missing on the sofa following the break-up of the Diamond–Owen team.

If Anne Diamond is the Queen of Camden, then the undoubted king is David Frost, whose *Frost On Sunday* show gets closest to the sort of programme the 'Famous Five' promised in their original manifesto. Frostie is equally comfortable chatting on an intellectual or 'man in the street' level, and has never ever been guilty of boring his audience. He is the only interviewer I know who could have drawn a 'you must be bonkers' response from Prime Minister Margaret Thatcher and still come up smiling and ready with the next question. David is the man we all feel that we can learn from at TV-am, and for a telly apprentice like me it is privilege to watch him at work. The best advice I got from the master was, 'Just be yourself, Jim. The camera will quickly catch you out if you try to put on an act.'

This is a reason I rarely use the dreaded Autocue at TV-am. I am convinced it takes any naturalness away from you. The most amazing bloke I've seen in front of a camera is Paul Gambaccini, who has a photographic memory. He rattles off complicated facts, figures and opinions on the music and movie scenes and everybody is convinced that he must be reading it on Autocue, but it all comes fresh out of his head.

The two best organised people I have worked with on the couch at Camden are jolly astrologer Russell Grant and that man of letters Gyles Brandreth, who got his education not only at Oxford but also at Yale (this old boy of Kingswood Secondary School, Hainault, is in awe of him). Both Russell and the garrulous Gyles have a prodigious output in the world of publishing and I sometimes wonder where they find their energy. I suppose Russell would tell me that it's all in the stars.

I often use the TV-am sofa as a soap box, and my tongue occasionally tows me into trouble. I had the meteorological office gunning for me in the autumn of 1987 when I described all television weather forecasters as 'useless ginks'. I was in the studio the day after they had failed to warn us about a hurricane that ripped through the south-east causing serious structural damage and destroying thousands of trees. I took my temper out on lovely TV-am weathergirl Trish Williamson, and said on air that she 'should be bloody well sacked.'

I didn't mean it, of course, and it's been good to see her progress to the job of forecaster for the national ITV weather team, but I would still rather rely on my own judgement looking at the sky than listen to some of the codswallop coming from the so-called experts. The more sophisticated they become with their computers the farther out they seem with their forecasts.

The nearest that I've ever come to thumping somebody on the TV-am set is when Mike Smith – the poor man's Noel Edmonds – suggested I was a small-minded bigot. His verbal dig came during a Camden Lock sofa discussion about a mess of an LWT show called *Trick or Treat*. I made the honest observation that I objected to the Saturday evening programme being shown at a time when children were obviously among the viewers. *Trick or Treat* was jointly hosted by Smith and a flamboyant, over-the-top gay called Julian Clary, also known as The Joan Collins Fan Club. My objection, and I was talking as a concerned grandfather, was that the gutter-style innuendo in the programme had no place on the screen during early evening television time. The tatty quiz show had already received destructive publicity for employing porn stars as hostesses, but I was more wound up by the performance of Clary, whom I described as a 'prancing poof'. I thought that it was disgraceful that he should go into the audience during what was allegedly a family show and ask such questions as, 'Have you picked up some rough trade on the way to the studio?'

There was a time when I would have smashed Mike Smith's teeth down his throat for his 'small minded bigot' crack. But my sober assessment of the situation as we sat glaring at each other on the TV-am sofa was that it was not worth the physical effort to make him famous.

Clary went on Michael Aspel's *Aspel and Company* chat show the following weekend and said I must have 'been on the bottle' when I made my comments. I didn't need defending, but Michael chose to point out, 'It must have been a milk bottle because Jim is off the booze.'

'He called me a prancing poof,' said Clary. 'My objection to that is that I don't prance. I've never pranced. I'm a mincer. I've always been a mincer.'

Clary is a very funny bloke if you like his sort of humour, and I had no objections to what he was saying on the Aspel show because it was screened late at night for an adult audience. He has since plumbed new depths with a send-up quiz show called *Sticky Moments,* but the fact that it goes out on Channel 4 at 10.30 at night at least puts his cheap innuendo out of sight and hearing of youngsters. I don't want to see him prancing around on my screen at a time when children are watching and wondering what on earth they are looking at. That doesn't make me bigoted, just a caring grandparent.

As if TV-am had not been through enough earthquaking crises in its short existence, there was an almighty fall-out in the winter of 1987 which proved fatal for 229 technicians who had been employed by the company. All members of the powerful Association of Cinematograph, Television and Allied Technicians (ACTT), they were said by fighting-mad Gyngell to be holding TV-am to ransom with excessive wage and expenses demands, and strangling it with restrictive practices. It was all an echo of what had recently been happening in Fleet Street where decades of domination by the printers had been ended by ruthlessly tough management.

Gyngell had been sparring with the union leaders for months, and I couldn't believe it when ACTT chose TV-am's Caring

Christmas campaign as their battle ground. Straight away they lost public sympathy as they went on strike to try to score what they thought would be a quick victory. But choosing to tangle with Gyngell was like walking into a Mike Tyson punch. He reacted by locking them out, and they were never allowed back inside the TV-am headquarters where they had all been enjoying the good life.

It is not for me to take sides, but it was heartbreaking to see so many of the good blokes I had become friendly with on the studio floor committing *harikari* by following senseless strike instructions. The hardest thing in the world was crossing their picket lines to get into the studio. It gave those of us in the National Union of Journalists – who voted overwhelmingly against strike action – a taste of what it must have been like to have been conscientious objectors during the war. I can say from bitter experience that it is much harder to cross a picket line than join it.

I am a union supporter to the point where common sense prevails, but once the brains-in-their-bums lefties start spreading their poison I find it difficult to suppress the patriotic right wing feelings that once took me into politics as a prospective Tory MP. It was back in 1972 just after I had finished my League playing career, and I failed to get the nomination for a constituency in Essex. Just as well, I suppose, because I was just starting out on the big boozing binge – not that 'The Problem' has stopped some politicians I could name making a career for themselves in the House.

Anyway, my feeling at the time of the TV-am strike was that the ACTT leaders must have been deaf, dumb and blind not to have learned the lessons of Wapping, where Rupert Murdoch – another iron-jawed Aussie – took on and destroyed the previously unbeaten print unions.

What knocked the wind out of the strikers is that TV-am managed to keep on the airways without them, and – even worse – actually increased the ratings. *Batman and Robin* came to the rescue, and the adventures of the caped crusaders lured near-record audiences for a station being run by a skeleton staff under the orchestration of the amazing Mr Gyngell.

It would have broken the hearts of the striking picket-line technicians if they could have seen the ease with which untrained secretaries and executives took to working the sophisticated studio equipment. As far as the viewers at home were concerned it was almost service as normal, and there was so much newspaper publicity about the strike that thousands of new viewers were being drawn to the programme out of curiosity.

Having made the decision to sack all of the strikers, Gyngell worked himself into the ground to keep TV-am ticking over. You only had to see the army of heavily muscled security men with which he surrounded himself and the TV-am studios to realise the pressure he was under in what had become as much a battle for pride and principles as profit.

The health of a workaholic can be just as much at risk as that of an alcoholic, and even a fitness freak like Bruce could not stand up to the sort of 15-hours-a-day working pace that he had set. His bill came in the shape of a heart attack just as it became clear that the strikers had been beaten. Gyngell had won his war, but very nearly at the cost of his life.

Within a handful of months the Pink Panther of the antipodes was back bounding through Egg Cup Towers dishing out advice on healthy living and the advantages of a good diet and quiet meditation.

Normal service had been resumed.

CHAPTER FOUR

I'm no saint

There are a procession of high-powered people in the world of television who will tell you that Greavsie's no saint. In fact I can sometimes be one of the most awkward cusses I know, and if I was a programme producer I would hate to have to deal with me. I've got a sort of cuddly, cheeky chappie image with the viewers, but the only part of me some TV bosses would like to cuddle is my windpipe.

Maybe it's a throwback to my days on the bottle, but there are some people who consider me a sort of Jekyll and Hyde character. There's the wise-cracking, relaxed guy you see on the TV screen, while off camera I can – just very occasionally – be a bit of a misery guts with a touchpaper temper.

I make this honest admission so that the people with whom I have fallen out can perhaps try to understand that I don't mean to lose control of my temper. It's just that I've got a fuse that is so short that it needs only a spark to ignite it, particularly if I feel hard done by. When I lose my temper I say that it's the O'Reilly coming out in me. O'Reilly was the name of my ancestors on my mother's side, southern Irish folk with magic in their tongues and, so the legend goes, wildness in their ways. It's from them that I have inherited my runaway tongue and my volatile temper (and perhaps what was my drinking habit).

Oh, really? No, O'Reilly!

A typical case of my temper zooming past boiling point came in the autumn of 1984 when I was in trouble for threatening to thump a milkman. We were trying the country life in a 15th century farmhouse that we had bought in the depths of Essex at Lindsell, near Great Dunmow. I was sitting with my feet up in my study when I heard a commotion coming from the drive leading up to the farm. I ran out to find Irene and my sons, Danny and Andy, in tears and screaming at the milkman, 'You've killed our dog.'

'What the hell's going on?' I shouted.

'The milkman's run over Wincey,' sobbed Irene.

(We had named the dog after animal-loving Wincey Willis at TV-am).

'You should have kept it under control,' said the milkman, who was standing by the side of his milkfloat.

The red mist came over my eyes and I threatened to clout him. 'Get off my land,' I yelled, adding a few raw adjectives. 'This is private property and I don't want you anywhere near it again. You can stick your milk.'

The milkman quickly departed and reported me to the police, who decided to take no action after getting my side of the story. If he had shown some small sign of remorse or sympathy I could have just about forgiven him, but his attitude made me blow my fuse. Nothing was going to bring our lovely collie back, and – as any dog owners will understand – he had broken our hearts. He did not realise how lucky he was to get away without a good hiding. A neighbour friend of mine came running on to the scene with his shotgun cocked, but that would have been taking it a bit too far.

The incident was so upsetting that we decided to jack in the good life in the country, and move back to the village world of Little Baddow. We had just forked out fifteen grand on a new roof, and I lost thousands on the sale while everybody else in the country was making massive profits on selling their homes.

Did I hear somebody say it's a funny old life?

It's in television where I have collected a reputation for being a bad-tempered git – not with my colleagues in front of the camera or with the camera crews and studio workers, but with the bosses. Right through my playing career I was never a lover of authority, and I was often the despair of managers with my attitude. I've taken this maverick outlook into television with me.

One of my biggest rows was with an old pal of mine, John Bromley, before the 1986 World Cup finals. I had known Brommers since he was a young local newspaper reporter in Essex and I was just starting out on my professional footballing career with Chelsea. He became a respected sports journalist on the *Daily Herald* and then the *Daily Mirror* before moving into television where he quickly rose to a top executive position with LWT.

It was Brommers who came up with the idea for the *Saint and Greavsie* show, and so I owe him a lot. But that didn't stop me blowing my top when I thought I was getting a lousy deal. When Brommers and his scheduling team were making plans for ITV's coverage of the 1986 World Cup finals in Mexico I put forward the idea that the Saint and I should introduce the show. I thought this would make a change from the tired format of Brian Moore fronting a panel of know-alls.

The reaction was that Greavsie had become a big head, and my idea got kicked into touch without serious consideration. Fair enough, I thought. Now I can spend the summer with my feet up. Then, purely by accident, I discovered that six *Saint and Greavsie* shows had been included in the World Cup schedule. I made it clear in no uncertain terms that I had no intention of taking part, particularly when I heard the money that was being offered. Brommers rang me at home and we had a furious row which ended with one of us putting down the phone. John insisted that it was me who hung up, and he complained about my attitude.

I was unhappy to fall out with Brommers, a marvellous administrator who has now departed from ITV Sport to take his talents to fresh fields. He was big enough to come back to me with a greatly improved appearance-money offer, and I climbed down and agreed to do the World Cup shows and also to appear as an occasional panel member.

A few bob, and you're anybody's, Greavsie!

Brian Moore did his usual thoroughly professional job shepherding the panellists through the preliminary matches before nipping off to Mexico to do what he is best at – commentating. Amazingly it was his first World Cup Final, and keeping him company as summariser was Kevin Keegan. In my opinion the programme planners should have sent Cloughie or the Saint to the Final (or even me!) rather than Keegan because they would have provided a better balance to Mooro's views.

I have to go on record here with an admission that Keegan has never been one of my favourite footballers. How he was twice voted European Footballer of the Year I will never know. I would give him ten out of ten for industry as a player, but no more than a mark of four out of ten for skill. I can name at least a dozen British forwards from the last 25 years who were a class above him. In fact, here are twenty names coming off the top of my head, and I could probably find another twenty if I looked into a record book for a memory jogger: George Best, Bobby Charlton, Denis Law, Roger Hunt, Geoff Hurst, Francis Lee, Peter Osgood, Rodney Marsh, Peter Thompson, Bryan Douglas, Johnny Byrne, Allan Clarke, Cliff Jones,

Jimmy Johnstone, Trevor Francis, Gary Lineker, Peter Beardsley, Ian Rush, John Barnes and – the great player who replaced Keegan at Liverpool – Kenny Dalglish.

I once came close to kicking in my television screen when I saw on ITV a programme called *Who's the Greatest?*, which was devised by my writing partner Norman Giller. I've said it to his face and I'll say it here in black and white: it was a lousy idea for a show. Past sporting heroes were compared with modern day stars, and a 12-person jury was asked to say who was the greater player after listening to evidence from star witnesses. In the programme that I watched, the jury voted by eleven votes to one that Kevin Keegan was a greater player than George Best. It is this opinionator's view that eleven members of that jury should have been hung. Michael Parkinson put the case for Best, and the Saint appeared as one of the witnesses along with Pat Jennings. Tom O'Connor, a blue-blooded Evertonian, argued on behalf of Keegan, with Trevor Brooking and Mike Channon as his expert witnesses. Parky said that the verdict had destroyed any faith he had in British sporting tastes. In a later programme Ian Rush was adjudged to have been a greater player than me. Going by the Best-Keegan decision, I saw the verdict as a compliment.

Kevin Keegan was not fit to tie George Best's bootlaces.

But I'm getting off my theme, and that is the Greavsie temper. According to Fleet Street it pushed me back into trouble again in the late summer of 1989, but I defy any father in the land to say he would not have reacted exactly as I did considering the provocation. I was the innocent party, but finished up with a black eye and looking the villain of the greatest farce in which I have ever been involved. But never for a moment did I lose my temper.

Irene was one of an army of volunteers who worked themselves into the ground to help raise money for the Sheiling Camphill School for disabled children by organising a charity pig roast in the private grounds of a house I used to own in the village of Little Baddow. I was roped in to grill and serve burgers and sausages for any kids who did not want to partake of the pig. It had been a happy gathering of caring families until suddenly it was turned into a nightmare. I am in no way making excuses for what occurred, but I just wonder how any father would react if he saw his daughter being thumped by a bloke. The person in question, a visitor to the charity event, had already insulted my son, Andy, in my hearing and I had politely suggested he kept his thoughts to himself. Andy had been clowning around on a nearby tennis court doing a John McEnroe impression purely for the entertainment of his partner and opponents in a knockabout doubles match.

Mitzi, my daughter, overheard the feller rubbishing Andy and – like any loving sister – spoke up for him. The next thing she had blood pouring down from her nose after this brave man had whacked her one. That's when I – still wearing my cooking apron – became involved, and suddenly it was like one of those *Dallas* barbecues where the Ewings and the Barnes's used to finish up brawling. I got caught by a sneak punch as I leapt to the defence of Mitzi. When it was all over Mitzi had a busted nose, I had a black eye and Irene had a broken heart. It was a harrowing experience, but it had nothing to do with the Greavsie temper. In fact it was because I *kept* my self control that the incident did not degenerate into something much worse.

Now I understand why several of my better-known friends who have celebrity status walk around with minders. They know they are sitting targets for publicity seekers, and make sure they keep certain types at arm's length. It convinced me that in future I should keep a low profile away from the television screen because I never again want to go through the torment and trauma triggered by that incident.

For the next few days I was plagued by photographers invading the privacy of my home to try to snatch pictures of my black eye. One newspaper accused me of brawling with a cameraman, which was an out-and-out lie.

But at least we managed to salvage some good out of it all. I sold an exclusive photograph of my shiner to *The Sun* in return for a £3,000 donation to the Camphill Trust.

I was once locked in a heated argument over money (what else?) with Central executive Andy Allan – a smashing bloke – when he suddenly stopped me in full flow and said, 'Jimmy, why the hell are you and I shouting at each other? You're the only star with whom I have this kind of verbal punch-up. And d'you know why?'

'Because I'm a pig-headed bastard,' I said.

'True,' said Andy. 'But the real reason is that it's because you should not be negotiating for yourself. For God's sake do what all the others do – get yourself an agent. That way you won't have to row with me. Leave it to an agent, and then you and I can remain pals.'

It was the best advice I ever got. I signed up with Barry Brown, a theatrical agent who now gets the sharp tongue treatment that I was using on other people. It's much better than taking it out on my television bosses, and they have started to like me just a little better since I began using Barry as my shield. I would recommend Barry to anybody who needs a negotiating representative (and for that plug, I want a percentage!). Barry does not quite know what to make of me. He says that he represents seventy actors and actresses and one novelty act, meaning me. It has been suggested that because he and I get on so well together we should form a double act. The suggested title: Allcock and Brown!

One person with whom I have never lost my temper is Ian St John, although my shifting moods mean that he is never 100 per cent sure of his footing with me (it was the same when I was steaming past him on the football pitch. Remember that 9–3 England-Scotland match, Saint?).

You're a nasty sod, Greavsie.

I had tremendous respect for Ian as a player with Liverpool and Scotland, but in those days I never really knew him as a person. He always seemed surrounded by showbiz types – Jimmy Tarbuck remains one of his closest pals – and I got the impression he was a bit of a flash git.

He came back into my life after suffering some hard times trying to establish himself as a manager and coach. Saint's coaching ability was highly thought of in the game, particularly at Coventry and at Sheffield Wednesday (where he was big Jack Charlton's right hand man). He put his head on the block as manager at Portsmouth, and still carries the scars of an unhappy ending to his managerial career when he was sacked without having really been given a proper chance to show what he could do.

Football's loss was television's gain. He had already proved his ability at the microphone when he reached the finals of a BBC competition to find a commentator. I thought he was the best by a mile, and he quickly confirmed that he was a television 'natural' when taking over from Brian Moore as presenter of *On the Ball*, which was the football slot on *World of Sport*.

I was invited to take part in a regular Saturday afternoon

cross-talk with Ian from the Birmingham studios while he was in London. I didn't fancy it one bit, but I was talked into it by Gary Newbon who convinced me it would be a good thing for my career. I think Gary now wishes he had kept his mouth shut, and then I might have remained a small time opinionator and not got too big for my boots.

Our long-distance chat became so popular that John Bromley proposed a full-blown *Saint and Greavsie* show in the LWT studios after *World of Sport* had been killed off. The way we work on the show is exactly how I used to play football. I leave The Saint to do all the hard graft – reading the Autocue and setting up all the inserts – while I just concentrate on slipping in and out of the action with hopefully funny one liners and comments on the main items. The Saint and I have been lucky in having imaginative editors at the helm in Bob Patience and then Richard Worth, and we have excellent input to the show from ITV team members – notably Martin Tyler, Alan Parry and Jim Rosenthal.

We set out to entertain and explain, in that order. We don't think the vast majority of our viewers want us blinding them with science about what is only a game. If we did have to get deadly serious about things, the Saint and I have 78 caps between us to prove that we know what we're talking about. Our bright and breezy approach means we have to take a lot of stick from some 'serious' sections of the media who think that we treat football too lightly. 'Saint and Greavsie are a couple of jokers who have managed to take football down to the level of a second-rate music hall act,' wrote one 'quality paper' scribe.

'I say, I say, I say, Saint, do you know why they call Scotland's goalkeeper Cinderella?'

'No, Greavsie. Why do they call Scotland's goalkeeper Cinderella?'

'Because he's always late for the ball.'

'I don't wish to know that. Kindly leave the page...'

I get most of the punchlines on the *Saint and Greavsie* show, but the Saint is a very funny man in his own right. We do the occasional personal appearance and Ian always goes down well with a sense of humour that can be as cutting as a claymore. In fact, on a golf course he has been known to slice a ball in two with his language! We get on well off as well as on the screen, but we don't suffocate each other. He lives happily as a family man up in the Wirral, and so we only see each other when we're working. We're not into each other's pockets (you would need a jemmy to get into the Saint's pocket). Morecambe and Wise were my favourite double act. The Saint is the wise man of our partnership, even down to the wig (he'll kick me in the kilt for letting on about that one!).

To wind the Saint up I get cheap laughs at the expense of Scottish goalkeepers, and I have almost made a career out of taking the mickey out of Scottish football, but I am a closet fan of the game in Scotland and I rate Rangers and Celtic on a par with Liverpool as the best organised and most successful clubs in Britain. And Hamilton Accies are the friendliest.

In fact just to prove how highly I rate the Jock footballers here is a team that I have selected from Scottish internationals of the last 25 years who I would back to beat most other combinations that you could come up with from the same era (I've given the clubs with which they were most identified during their careers):

Ronnie Simpson (Newcastle and Celtic)
Sandy Jardine (Rangers)
Danny McGrain (Celtic)
Pat Crerand (Celtic and Manchester United)
Billy McNeill (Celtic)
Dave Mackay (Hearts and Tottenham)
Jimmy Johnstone (Celtic)
Kenny Dalglish (Celtic and Liverpool)
Denis Law (Manchester City and Manchester United)
Jim Baxter (Rangers)
John Robertson (Nottingham Forest)
Subs: **Billy Bremner** (Leeds United)
John Greig (Rangers)
Graeme Souness (Liverpool)

I would make my old Tottenham pal Dave Mackay the skipper. He was the most inspiring player ever to set foot on a football field during my playing days, and just his presence on the pitch had the effect of making his team-mates feel taller.

There is no way I can let this topic go without trying to select an all-English team to beat my Scottish All Stars. Again, I have made my selection from internationals of the past 25 years. The only position in which I have 'swallowed' it is at goalkeeper where I have not been able to decide between Gordon Banks and Peter Shilton. I always rated Banksie the greatest England goalkeeper of my era, with Irish master Pat Jennings just a fingertip ahead of him. But Shilts, who had to live in the shadow of Banks when he first started out on his career, has put together a tremendous case to be considered the greatest of all goalkeepers (*Who's the Greatest?* Now there's an idea for a television series!)

This is my England selection:

Gordon Banks or **Peter Shilton**
Jimmy Armfield (Blackpool)
Ray Wilson (Huddersfield and Everton)
Bryan Robson (Manchester United)
Roy McFarland (Derby County)
Bobby Moore (West Ham)
Glenn Hoddle (Tottenham)
Gary Lineker (Leicester, Everton and Tottenham)
Bobby Smith (Tottenham)
Johnny Haynes (Fulham)
Bobby Charlton (Manchester United)
Subs: **Nobby Stiles** (Manchester United)
Alan Ball (Everton and Arsenal)
Paul Gascoigne (Newcastle and Tottenham)

That's right – there's no place in my team for Kevin Keegan, or for Chris Waddle, whose £4 million-plus transfer fee proved that the football world has gone bonkers.

Bobby Moore would be my skipper, and I include Gary Lineker in the attack because I rate him the finest English striker of the last 20 years. There is a school of thought that I am anti-Lineker because I stated that he would never be quite the same force following the attack of hepatitis that sidelined him when he was playing with Barcelona. Hepatitis was the illness that robbed me of a yard of speed when I was at my peak, and I think it has had a similar anchoring effect on Gary. But he has been intelligent enough to make slight adjustments to his game, making his mark with clever positional play rather than the old explosive burst of speed.

Now where was I before I rudely interrupted myself? Oh yes, the *Saint and Greavsie* show. I tread a tightrope on the programme when one trip of the tongue can cause a lot of damage (or damages), and because it's live the ITV lawyers watch with legal-eagle eyes in case I drop myself, and them, in it. I was in it up to my neck following one match in which I said that the referee had sent off a player just to get himself into history before he retires. The referee hit me with a writ for libel, and I was forced to apologise for my unwise remark in the High Court and had to pick up the bill for his legal costs and also make a payment to the Referees' Association Benevolent Fund.

I mention this best-forgotten case here as an illustration of how careful you need to be when shooting from the lip with opinions. I have tried to become more guarded with my comments, making sure that I add 'in my opinion' when passing judgments. You are into a minefield when you start making an opinion sound like a statement of fact.

It's not *that* easy being an opinionator.

I have been lucky enough to have received three *TV Times* awards, which is a measure that I must have been doing something right. Those awards – and the beauty of them is that they are decided by the public – have given me the greatest pleasure of my middle-age years, apart from the arrival of seven smashing grandchildren. I never once won an individual award in football, so to do it in a field in which I was a rank novice filled me with enormous pride. I know that sounds corny, but it's true.

To be honest, I have got more satisfaction out of my television career than I did as a footballer. I'm not saying that I didn't enjoy my playing career, but I was one of those jammy sods to whom playing football and scoring goals came naturally. I never had to sweat at the game. I was always able to play it off the cuff, much to the dismay and frustration of coaches who wanted me to fit into their plans like some sort of robot.

But in the world of television I have had to learn as I go along. Everything I have done has been because of the concentration and effort that I have put into it. A lot of kind and considerate people have helped me, but I know in my heart that I've managed to make a success of my career to date by my own efforts. I have needled a lot of people on my way, but I hope they accept that it is because of my passion for my new career – a passion that a lot of people thought I lacked as a footballer.

The *TV Times Awards* shows are always among the best organised of all the British Oscar-style ceremonies. Lee Majors, famous for his role as *The Six Million Dollar Man* Steve Austin, was guest of honour at the first show where I received an award. I'm not sure he knew he was there, suffering as he was from a severe form of jet lag. Father and son stunt men Nosher and Greg Powell were placed in the audience to stage a sham fight with Lee, and when they jumped him as he made his way to the stage a table went flying along with glasses and a bottle of wine. It was spectacular stuff, and what amused me was that by the time the Six Million Dollar Man got to the stage to receive his award he was breathing as heavily as somebody who had just been three rounds with Mike Tyson.

It was even funnier at the *TV Times Awards* show the previous year when I was a member of the audience. Bruce Forsyth was co-hosting the show with Nanette Newman, and the star guest lined up for the finale was Robert Mitchum. Bruce did a marvellous presentation job, but with just Mitchum left to come on stage he had the sort of blank we all dread on 'live' television. He appeared to forget completely about Mitchum standing in the wings and went straight into the final wind-up script, thanking everybody for coming and saying how much he had enjoyed it all. It took a few seconds for Nanette Newman to realise that Bruce was closing the show, and she and the bewildered floor manager managed to attract his attention and remind him that he had yet to introduce the night's big star.

Like a true pro, Bruce made it all seem part of the act and he switched from a closing speech to an introduction for 'one of the great stars of Hollywood'. I was helpless with laughter just thinking of Mitchum standing in the wings wondering what the hell was going on as he listened to Bruce saying good night to the viewers before he had got on stage.

'Have I already been on?' you can imagine the Hollywood veteran thinking to himself in panic. 'God, I can't remember a damn thing about it!'

When he finally made his entrance he looked like a man in a trance. It was my turn to have the on-camera panic feeling a few days later when I was in the TV-am studio with dear old Tommy Trinder, who I had known for years because of his close connection with football (well with Fulham, which I suppose has got loose connections with the game). Tommy's brainbox – it was the sharpest I had ever known when he was at his peak as a comedian – had gone a bit, and he was not really sure what he was doing in the studio for what was to prove one of his last screen appearances before he passed on in the summer of 1989. I was to interview him in the *After Nine* slot about television in the 1950s, and for an hour before we went on air I rehearsed with him what I was going to ask him. Entertainments editor Jason 'I've booked 'em all' Pollock and my righthand man Joe Steeples helped me warm Tommy up and remind him of the era we were about to discuss. He was as bright as a button before we were called to the studio, telling us a string of hilarious anecdotes about his days as the first compere of *Sunday Night at the London Palladium.*

He told us about one top-line star who was so heavily into the spirit bottle before she went on stage that Tommy told the stagehands, only half jokingly, 'For gawd's sake don't light a fag near her or we'll all go up.'

'That's the sort of thing we want from you, Tom,' I said with enthusiasm. 'Just tell a couple of those stories when you're on the sofa and it will make a marvellous spot.'

We gave Tommy the big build-up that he deserved, and I had got him nicely primed for the first question, which was: 'Tell us about *Sunday Night at the London Palladium*, Tom. What do you recall of the first ever show?'

You can imagine my reaction when Tommy replied: 'What I want to know is what Terry Wogan's up to?'

'Uh, Terry Wogan?' I said, trying to stop my mouth from moving in a goldfish style. 'He's got a chat show, of course, but he never appeared on those early *Sunday Night at the London Palladium* shows. What were they like?'

'He's not asked me on the show, you know,' said Tommy. 'Gawd knows why. He never seems to be off the screen. Have you been on his show?'

'No, Tom,' I said suddenly feeling in need of a drink. 'Umm, but I would have loved to have appeared on *Sunday Night at the London Palladium.* Let's have a look at this little clip of one of the early shows. I'm sure it will revive happy memories.'

I managed to get Tommy back on to some sort of track when we came out of the clip, but those first few moments were the scariest – and also the most hilarious – I've known on television.

It should have been warning enough about the problems of hosting a chat show, but my ego insisted that I answer the challenge when it came my way.

My temper was about to tow me into more trouble.

CHAPTER FIVE

Chat and that

This Is Your Life scriptwriter Roy Bottomley came up with an imaginative idea for a chat show. The scenario he had in his mind was of a kitchen set in the studio, with celebrities dropping in for a cuppa and a chat. A general handyman – somebody like Frank Bruno – would act as a resident straight man, and there would be a busy yet relaxed atmosphere. There was only one thing wrong with Roy's idea. He planned the format around *me* as the host.

Let me start at the beginning. In 1987 Central gave me my own chat show in the Midlands. It was run on a shoestring budget, and I interviewed ordinary people who had done extraordinary things. It was not a million miles removed from the theme of the *People* show launched by Derek Jameson on BBC and then taken over by my old sparring partner Bruno. The sort of thing I went in for was chatting to two members of the Official Monster Raving Looney political party about their manifesto for the next general election, talking to the captain of the QE2 and, on the same show, interviewing a transvestite who was a respectable pillar of society.

It was all very low-key but interesting, and we had a terrific little production team under the guidance of young producer Nick Rowan and director Timothy Moores. Roving reporter John Swallow gave the programme a lift with amusing off-beat Whicker-type cameos from around the country. The public seemed to like it and one Sunday newspaper critic got carried away to the point of describing me as the new Terry Wogan (I personally was very happy with the old one, who I rate on a par with Parky and Michael Aspel as king of the chat show hosts).

Confession time. My success on the show gave me big ideas that I could do a Wogan-style job, and the Central executives seemed to share my inflated opinion. They put up the idea of a networked Greavsie chat show, and the rest of the companies in ITV's complicated set-up agreed to give it a go. For some

The two footballing faces of Jim. That's me on the left just starting out on my career as a 17-year-old with Chelsea.

Above: As I looked in the peak years of my career with Tottenham.

Top left: A superb study of one of my more memorable goals when I managed to roll a shot into the Burnley net from the edge of the penalty area in the third minute of the 1962 FA Cup Final at Wembley. Happy days.

Bottom left: These are some of the footballing prizes I used to proudly show off in the summertime of my career when goals were my business. If you were to walk into my home now you would not see one of them displayed. They are strictly for the memory. If you look hard at the centre of the picture you will see the reflection of one of my better prizes . . . it's my son, Andy, then aged four and not realising that he was ruining the photographer's carefully composed shot.

Above: What a rogues' gallery! It's England's old Old Stars trying to make some bread at the back end of our careers. We have just arrived in Toronto to play in a 1973 indoor tournament arranged by former Scottish have-boots-will-travel inside-forward Ken Chisholm (pictured left). Keeping me company are 1966 World Cup heroes Gordon Banks, Bobby Moore and Jack O'Charlton.

Above: Having a ball with me are two all-time greats who were among my team-mates in Toronto, the Portuguese panther Eusebio and, of course, the one and only Banksie.

Right: Boxer Billy Walker just might be giving five good reasons why Prime Minister Harold Wilson (that's him with his pipe on the left) and I should take shares in his baked potato restaurant business. We were guests of the PM at No. 10 in 1965 when Billy was the golden boy of British boxing and I was England's top goalscorer. It was around about then that Billy and his older, smarter brother George started their baked potato business that has now grown into a multi-million pound company.

I was very much into businesses myself in the mid-Sixties, but I managed to booze the profits away. Well done Greavsie!

The drinking days, not that I always had such distinguished company when I was knocking it back. I am celebrating Tottenham's 3–1 1962 FA Cup Final victory over Burnley with skipper Danny Blanchflower (centre) and my old sidekick Bobby Smith.

Screenmaster Sean Connery, taking a break from filming the James Bond classic 'You Only Live Twice' at Pinewood Studios during the 1966 World Cup. We're both a little thinner on top and I reckon that we've both lived more than twice!

I'm sharing a glass with actor Leslie Phillips, also while at Pinewood. When I was really hitting the bottle I preferred to drink alone. That way I did not waste any time talking.

What a difference ten years makes! That's me the weekend that I admitted publicly that booze was killing me. I'm not a pretty sight, am I?

Ten years on I am toasting a decade on the wagon. When the advertisers see this I am expecting a rush of offers for me to appear in a coffee commercial. I drink gallons of the stuff.

reason Central chose to bring in an outside producer rather than trust the team that had done so well for me in my Midlands-only show. The man they turned to was Richmond-based Roy Bottomley, one of the most experienced writers in television. He is a former Fleet Street journalist whose many credits – during a long partnership with another scriptwriter called Tom Brennand – included the classic comedy series *Nearest and Dearest* and the hard-hitting TV drama series *Man at the Top*. But he is best known as the power behind the throne on *This Is Your Life*, working as number one writer to Eamonn Andrews for more than 20 years before teaming up with Michael Aspel.

I worked with Roy's young reporter son, Steve, at TV-am before he switched to Sky, but I had never met 'old man' Bottomley in my life. Norman Giller was No 2 writer to him on *This Is Your Life* and described him as 'one of the best professionals I have ever worked with.' That was good enough for me, and Norm arranged for us to get together over lunch at a Heathrow hotel where Roy outlined his idea for a restyled Greavsie chat show.

For starters, Roy explained the kitchen chat-and-cuppa format. 'The impression the viewer will get is that people are dropping into your place for a cup of tea and a natter,' he said. 'I'm hoping to get Frank Bruno as a resident straightman for you. He can wander into the kitchen as a general handyman, perhaps flooding you in one show when trying his hand at plumbing.'

'Great idea, Roy,' I said.

For the main course, Roy explained his 'star dust' theory. 'I've seen recordings of your Central chat show,' he said, trying without success to keep a look of disdain off his face. 'By just talking to ordinary people you cannot help but have an ordinary show. That won't do for network television. We want star dust, and I have the contacts to make sure you get good names on the show.'

'I don't want it becoming a plugger's paradise,' I said. 'The screen is already stuffed with so-called stars talking about their latest book, their latest record, their latest film, their latest show. It's so bloody boring.' (I was not to know that a little over a year later I would be looking for shows on which I could plug *this* book! I promise to try not to be boring. Any offers?).

For dessert, Roy filled me in with fascinating stories about his life in television which would make a book that is well worth plugging. His version of our chat show fiasco will make particularly interesting reading. My favourite story from his huge collection of amusing anecdotes is of when he accompanied Eamonn Andrews to Hollywood to trap Dudley Moore for *This Is Your Life*. While in California they were having a drink in their hotel suite with one of the most glamorous of all Hollywood actresses. She said in Eamonn's hearing, 'God, I could do with some coke.' Being a gentleman, Eamonn called room service and ordered a Coca Cola for her. When he handed her the drink, she looked at Eamonn as if he was mad and said, 'That's not quite the coke I had in mind.' To lovely, innocent Eamonn the world of drugs was a foreign world and he said to her, 'I don't think they've got any Pepsi.'

Anyway, my ego allowed me to be lured into accepting Roy's creative concept for a chat show, although I secretly harboured doubts about it. I felt in my bones that I would be much more comfortable chatting to ordinary people with interesting stories to tell.

Come on, Greavsie. You used to be a piss-artist, now you're a pessimist. You can do it. After all, you're the new Wogan!

We produced three shows for the eyes of Midlands audiences only before we went on to the national network. They were three collectors items. I made a right pig's ear of them all, and my short-lived friendship with Roy Bottomley quickly turned to enmity as I looked around for somebody to blame for the shambles. If we had put them out as comedy shows we might have topped the ratings because I was stumbling around the kitchen set as if I'd been hitting the cooking wine.

I suddenly realised that I was being asked to do a job that was beyond my capabilities. The chatting was the easy part. I find it easy to rabbit to people, but I was being strangled by what I thought were the restrictions of Roy's script that called on me to be almost as much an actor as a chat show host. Just about the only gift I've got – apart from the gab – is the ability to be natural in front of a camera. But now I was having to work off the dreaded Autocue, and I was staring at it so wide-eyed that people no doubt thought that I was legless as well! All my life I had survived by doing things off the cuff – on the football pitch and in my new career in television. Now I felt as trapped as a prisoner as I tried to spout somebody else's words.

From being a striker having to worry only about putting the

ball into the net, I suddenly found myself cast in the role of a midfield schemer. I was having to remember to cue video-tape inserts, which questions to ask which guest – there were as many as six of them to each of the early programmes – and also to answer the doorbell and when to make a telephone call. All of this in twenty-five minutes. My old pal Frank Bruno had pulled out of his proposed 'live' appearances as my resident straight man because he was in training for a big show of his own with Mike Tyson. So we went through the charade of me pretending to make a telephone call to him each week while he gave pre-recorded answers to my questions. It was so stiff and stilted that one critic wrote: 'I thought I had tuned into a repeat of *The Woodentops*.' Frank and I looked like our *Spitting Image* dummies!

Pat Roach, memorable as 'Bomber' in *Auf Wiedersehen Pet*, was employed as the handyman for the first show which went out live. There was one unintentionally hilarious incident when I went to the sink to fill a kettle so that I could make a cup of tea for my guests (yes, we were that much into realism). The tap had not been fixed properly, and as I turned it on it came off in my hand. Water was shooting everywhere and big Pat, a professional wrestler when not acting, had to use all his strength to turn off the water with a spanner. He was a really handy handyman. There was a large pool of water on the floor through which all my guests had to tread. And, yes, I was feeling out of my depth.

I had Joe Steeples – my good pal at TV-am – working with me as programme associate. Joe must have thought he had become the invisible man because almost every idea he put up to try to improve the show seemed to be ignored. There were so many guests crowding on to the set that I was not able to give any of them the individual attention they deserved. Freddie Trueman, for instance, came on during the scandal of England's cricketers being accused of hanky panky with hotel barmaids. Freddie is a great raconteur and had some fascinating stories to tell about the off-the-field antics of past England players, but I was only allowed a couple of minutes with him and so he was left like an unexplored gold mine.

The critics had a field day at my expense, cutting me off at the legs and more than making up for all the encouraging things they had written about my early TV appearances. Everybody had been so kind and supportive when I was clawing my way back up after my drink problem, but now they seemed to be taking some sort of delight in knocking me back down again. I felt as if I was being tackled by an army of Norman Hunters. 'It's painful to watch Jimmy Greaves looking into the wrong cameras and searching blindly for his prompt cards,' commented one poison-pen critic, 'I was hoping a referee would walk on and show him the red card.' I had dished it out as a critic. Now I was having to take it on the chin. It don't 'alf hurt, mum!

I could see my new career going up in flames, and I called my agent Barry Brown and told him to get me out of the contract before I made a fool of myself nationwide. Bob Southgate was the executive producer of the show, and I wanted Barry to tell him that either Roy Bottomley went or I did. He sensibly talked me into seeing the job through. 'Put it all down to experience,' he said. 'Just try to relax and be yourself. If you were to pull out now you would get a reputation for being unreliable.'

While all this was going on I made one of the dafter decisions of my life. I moved to Cornwall.

Irene and I had bought a flat in Cornwall overlooking Falmouth Harbour. We spent a few days down there each month and fell head-over-heels in love with the place. 'I know,' I said, 'let's buy a house down here and move to Cornwall for good.' It was just about the silliest thing I had said since, 'I know, let's move to Milan . . .'

The property market was buoyant at the time, and in just a matter of weeks we had sold our home in Little Baddow and had bought a picturesque house overlooking the River Helford in the beautiful setting of Helford Passage, just a few miles from where my daughter, Lynn, was helping to run an estate agency business. We thought we had found our dream house, but were just about to walk into a nightmare.

The hardest wrench was giving up my twice-weekly spot on TV-am where I felt like one of the family.

But what the hell. I'm going to be the new Wogan.

Timing it like a master, I managed to organise one of the most disruptive moves of my life so that it virtually co-incided with the first of my 12-week run of chat shows. 'It will be no problem,' I said to Irene (who was lumbered with all the moving headaches). 'I can get to the Birmingham studios quicker from Cornwall than from Essex.'

Famous last words. Given a clear run I could have made the 270-mile drive to the studios in about four hours. I rarely did it in better than five hours, and sometimes took more than six hours. All it needed was one caravan or a tractor on the Cornwall roads and I was trapped. I knew within a week of the move that I had made a right cock-up, but I kept it to myself because I did not want to upset Irene. Meantime, Irene had also realised that we had got it wrong but she kept it to herself because she did not want to upset me while my mind was full of the challenge of the chat show. So there we were both kidding to each other that we loved our new home.

We had been full-time in the West Country for about five weeks when Irene and I sat glumly looking out of the window at a rain mist that had reduced visibility to about twenty yards. Our moods matched the weather. 'I don't know how to say this, love,' I said, 'but this just isn't right. I think we've got to get back to Essex where we belong.'

Irene sighed with relief. 'I feel exactly the same way,' she said, 'but I didn't want to be the one to say it.

I felt as if a ton weight had been lifted off my shoulders, and we started immediately making plans for our escape from paradise. We were surrounded by stunning scenery, but we quickly realised that a view, is a view, is a view. It was a lovely place to retire to, but we had impetuously got down there at least fifteen years too early. The local people in our village of Mawnan Smith went out of their way to make us feel welcome, but we just could not help feeling like onlookers rather than being part of it all.

Within twenty-four hours our house was up for sale, and just three weeks later we sold and were back on the road to Essex. Our move to paradise had lasted two months. We returned to Little Baddow and found a home to tide us over until we could get the time to look for a place in which to finally settle down. It was just as if we had not been away, and I told people that we had been on holiday to Cornwall with the slight difference that we had taken our furniture with us.

It was a devastating time for me. My dear old Dad died of a heart attack at the age of eighty while we were in Cornwall, and I got emotionally upset when I thought of all the good times we'd had when I was a kid first stepping out on the football trail. Dad had been an excellent sportsman in his youth, and had played good-class football, hockey and tennis during Army service in India in the 1930s; and when he returned home he used to turn out for three different local football clubs a week. Dad used to stud and dubbin my boots for me while Mum would wash and iron my kit. More importantly, Dad spent hours making sure I could kick as accurately with my right foot as my natural left foot. My success in football gave Dad as much pleasure as my descent into alcoholism gave him pain, but never once did he show me anything less than his full support and I know that he was proud of the way I pulled myself out of the pit into which I had fallen. I had spoken to Dad while he had sitting in his garden in Hainault just a short time before his heart attack. He had recalled his happy times as a tube train driver on the Central Line and talked fondly about the days 'when they played football the way it should be played.' He was content in his retirement years, and that is how I want to remember him.

What with Dad passing on, the catastrophe of the Cornwall move, and endless traffic jams and the strain being put on me by the problems of the chat show, I was ready to blow. And it was Roy Bottomley who was going to feel the full force of my uncorked temper.

By the time of the fourth chat show – and several heated clashes with Roy over the format – we had brought some semblance of order to the programme. All the 'business' of me wandering around the kitchen as if it was my second home went out of the window. Apart from a walk-to-camera opening to the show, I was all but nailed on a kitchen stool so that I could talk to my guests around a table. One of the jokes flying behind my back was that I was the Gerald Ford of chat show hosts, unable to walk and chew gum at the same time. I didn't mind the jokes, but I did mind having so many people to chat to that the kitchen at times resembled Piccadilly in the rush hour. We cut back the invitations to a maximum of four, which was just about manageable in the time that we had on air.

Having realised that I was not exactly a master of the Autocue, Roy kept my reading cues right down and I started to work from notes on small prompt cards. He also shut off everybody's voice in my earpiece apart from his own as he searched for the best way to bring the naturalness back into my performance. But I was still not happy over some of the guest bookings that he was making. We had gone down the 'plug' hole just like so many of the other chat shows. Anita Dobson came on and plugged a record and a show. Kim Wilde came on and plugged a record and her part in the Michael Jackson tour. Britt Ekland came on and plugged a film. Penny Junor came on and plugged a paperback book. They were all smashing guests, but it was not the sort of show that I wanted.

What angered me most of all was that I thought Roy was booking too many leggy girls purely for decoration on the show. Linda Lusardi came on and gave me an excellent interview about her ambition to lose her Page 3 image and turn to serious acting, but several of the girls who called into the kitchen had little to contribute apart from their looks. What it boiled down to, basically, was that Roy wanted glamour while I wanted guests who had some depth. This is the issue that finally made me snap with Roy. We were in the bar at the hotel where he was staying close by the studios when I unloaded on him. I cannot remember everything I said, but I do recall that at one stage during the red mist period I had hold of him by the tie and could have throttled him. 'If you book one more bloody bimbo,' I shouted, 'you can f***ing well interview her yourself because I'll be in my car on the way home.'

My temper was out of control, and luckily programme director David Millard was there to cool me down, otherwise I might have done something to Roy Bottomley that we would have both regretted.

I have to give Roy full marks for the way he reacted to my threat of physical assault. He calmly straightened his tie and said, 'Don't pussyfoot about, Jim. Why don't you say what you really mean!'

It was stupid of me to tackle Roy in a public place and somebody who saw our shouting match tipped off a Fleet Street newspaper and reported that I had been rolling drunk. I was not pissed – just pissed off. Anyway, I had delivered my message loud and clear, and from that day on we got on much better. I think Roy would agree that we did not have the right chemistry between us. In a way I feel guilty because his original kitchen-and-cuppa chat show idea was excellent, and I should have been right upfront with him when he first outlined it and told him that it was a great idea . . . but for somebody else, not for me. I believe that Roy and I would have got on much better in the good old bad old days when I loved a pint or three. After each show Roy liked to exercise his elbow with the production team in the green room, and I sensed he thought that I was showing less than total commitment by disappearing immediately after the programmes to get home to Irene. Since kicking the bottle, I have always made it a rule to try to avoid unnecessary temptations – and there are few places as tempting as a green room. In my thirsty days I could have drunk it dry.

The green room is the hospitality – or hostility – area in which guests and programme staff relax before and after shows. There are dozens of stories about celebrities disgracing themselves in green rooms where a well-stocked bar is always the focal point. My favourite green room story was told to me by that much-missed comic genius Eric Morecambe. He came to the LWT studios to add his unequalled comedy touch to the coverage of the 1982 World Cup finals. We stood together in, of all places, the green room and each of us ordered a Perrier water. Eric told me that he had read the book about my drinking excesses, *This One's On Me*, and that it had helped convince him that he had to cut down on the hooch. Talking of drink led Eric to this hilarious tale: 'Ernie and I were recording one of our early shows and we had a distinguished old actor playing a walk-on role in one of our sketches. He had been a top-line star at his peak, but – as with so many people in our profession – he liked the hard stuff too much for his own good. He was brought to the studio in a courtesy car, and after a rehearsal he found his way into the green room. We had a few technical delays and he had time to get himself nicely plastered. When the time came for us to record the sketch he could not be found anywhere, and we had to do a quick rewrite and go ahead without him. One of our programme assistants telephoned the old boy's agent to tell him that we had "lost" his star. The worried agent called his home and our hero himself answered. It transpired that he had wandered out of the studio and back to the courtesy car where he decided to have a quick doze. The driver found him asleep in the back, assumed that he had finished his work and drove him home. The old boy vaguely remembered the rehearsal, convinced himself that it must have been the real thing and had no idea he had "gone missing" until his agent rang him.'

I creased up with laughter, and dear old Eric pushed his spectacles sideways. 'This boy's a fool,' he announced to the bar. 'One Perrier water and he'll believe anything.'

Eric Morecambe. They'll never be another like him.

We got into a reasonable rhythm by about the halfway point in the chat show series, and the ratings were satisfactory without being sensational. One newspaper slanderously reported that the show was such a flop that Thames had decided to axe it after just two weeks. That was a downright lie. Thames had decided months in advance to run a series of feature films in the Tuesday evening spot that I was occupying, and they had already allotted me a place in their Thursday evening schedules. The show was not axed but transferred. In their mischievous report, the newspaper quoted an unnamed Thames executive as saying, 'His latest show is rubbish – simply hopeless.' I can take anything that the Press dish out, except when it is completely fabricated. Eric Morecambe gave me advice about Press criticism. He told me, 'Enjoy the nice things they write, and ignore the nasty stuff. If you complain you will just give them a satisfaction they don't deserve. I learnt the hard way because Ernie and I had to take some terrible stick early in our careers. I remember one critic wrote during our first television series, "What's a television? Answer: The box in which they buried Morecambe and Wise." I wasted time worrying about what that man wrote, but the public obviously felt otherwise. Just satisfy yourself that you are doing your best.'

I was far from satisfied that I had done my best in the early chat shows, but once I began to relax and had less of a load to carry I started to almost enjoy the experience. When it was all over I vowed never to do another chat show, but I have served the toughest possible apprenticeship and now that the bruises have healed I would not mind another go – but without the 'star dust'. Joe Steeples and I have got an idea for a new style chat show in which I would literally talk to the man in the street. Nine times out of ten you will find it is the ordinary person who has the most extraordinary story to relate. Knock on any door and you will find somebody with an interesting tale to tell.

Having sat in the hot seat, I am more than ever in awe of the likes of Terry Wogan and Michael Aspel, who conduct their chat shows with an apparent air of relaxation that puts each of their guests at ease and encourages excellent responses to their questions. The viewer is never allowed to suspect that there might have been last-minute panic off camera. I remember our biggest worry was when Peter Howitt – then the heart-throb star of *Bread* – got stuck in a traffic jam and arrived literally minutes before he had to walk on to the set. In a way it worked to our advantage because Peter and I were able to chat away without the hindrance of planted questions. One guest who we knew would not have any problems with the traffic was Joe Brown. He flew from London to Birmingham in his own private plane.

When the chat show series finally ended, Roy – my old sparring partner – called a team meeting, and presented me with a football signed by everybody on the production staff. It was a really thoughtful gesture, and it made me feel guilty about some of the wobblies that I had thrown in the fraught, early days when I feared that I had made the mistake of a lifetime in agreeing to do the show.

If Roy reads this I want him to know I didn't mean the things I said to him in temper (well, not all of them). What I suggest that we do is sit down and co-write a comedy series based on our experiences putting the chat show together. It would be even funnier than *Nearest and Dearest*.

I'll say this for Roy Bottomley – he at least did not order me to wear a sponsored sweater, which is the cue for the background story to yet another Greavsie bust-up.

I was about to cause a scene in the green room.

CHAPTER SIX

V-necks and V-signs

For years the ITV bosses had eyed BBC's *A Question of Sport* with envy, particularly its consistent appearance in the Top 20 ratings. Central were convinced they had discovered a quiz show to rival it when Birmingham-based comedian Don MacLean and some associates came up with the format for *Sporting Triangles*. Critics claimed that it was just a rip-off of *A Question of Sport*, but there were enough differences to give it an identity and standing of its own.

For a start, there were three teams competing rather than two and this called for the engagement of three resident captains. Here comes the conceited Greavsie again: I had wanted to be the questionmaster because I really fancied myself in the David Coleman role, but the show's executive producer Gary Newbon – my boss on Central Sport – didn't think I was suited to it. So I settled for being one of the captains. I was delighted to be involved because I have always been a keen sports fan, and pride myself on a reasonable all-round knowledge (and the appearance money wasn't bad!). Andy Gray, the cheerful Jock who has been a footballing idol in the Midlands with Aston Villa and Wolves, was selected as one of my rivals after several experiments, and 1984 Olympic javelin gold medallist Tessa Sanderson was an imaginative third choice.

A major difference between *Sporting Triangles* and its well established rival on BBC is that it is very much a high tech programme, with heavy reliance on computer input. A pilot show, with Don MacLean as one of the captains, worked well enough to encourage the network to give the go ahead for a series. Nick Owen was recalled to his old Birmingham stamping ground as the question master.

I rate Nick one of the better presenters on television, but he had his hands and head so full of complicated instructions to tie in with the needs of the computer that he was never his usual relaxed self in the first series. He ran the show with a headmasterish attitude instead of treating it as a bit of fun. I tried to get some banter going with him but it was heavy work. The pace of the show suffered because of the interminable time we had to wait for the computerised dice to move around the triangle board to decide which questions we would be asked. Another major error was that the questions were pitched at sporting mastermind level rather than at the punters at home. It is a mistake that *A Question of Sport* never makes, which is why it has always had such strong family appeal and has been such a success.

It was particularly tough on Tessa, whose sports knowledge away from her specialist subject of athletics was very weak. She had to rely heavily on her guest partners and the before-programme coaching from producer Jeff Farmer, a former top Midlands sports journalist whose enthusiasm and expertise steered the programme past rocks that could easily have sunk it. But we could all forgive Tessa anything when she lit up the screen with her lovely smile. I admired her guts at the way she pushed herself back into the public spotlight after the sort of unnerving experience that would have broken the heart of somebody with less character. My writing partner Norman Giller had been putting together a script for a *This Is Your Life* tribute to Tessa when he was ordered to drop it. The *Life* office at Thames had received poison pen letters making sick allegations about Tessa's private sex life and accusing her of having boosted her javelin throwing by taking drugs. Tessa said that she knew who was behind the mud-throwing campaign, and that she had wept buckets to think that anybody could stoop so low. She is a full-of-fun girl, a dedicated athlete and she brightens any company that she is in. I would not like to have the conscience of the sick person who tried (and failed) to ruin her with lies and innuendo.

Anyway, *Sporting Triangles* limped into a second series by which time we had got into our stride. A lot of the early faults had been ironed out and we started to collect a following. We were not challenging the ratings supremacy of *A Question of Sport*, but the improvement in the content was noticeable. Nick Owen had loosened up and got into the spirit of the show, and it had become entertaining.

Across the channel at BBC David Coleman and his team at least knew they had to look over their shoulders. The best thing they had going for them was the rapport between the rival captains, cuddly Bill Beaumont and giggly Emlyn Hughes.

One critic described them as the BBC's answer to Saint and Greavsie.

Sporting Triangles had gained sufficient popularity to warrant a third series in 1989. A press conference was called to reveal that Andy Craig, a popular presenter in the Midlands, was taking over as the question master. Nick Owen had committed himself to another quiz called *Hit Man*, and I'm told it was a real moneybags job. Good luck to him, I say. I felt as if I was the target of a hit man when from right out of the blue it was announced that Emlyn Hughes was joining *Sporting Triangles* as replacement for Tessa Sanderson as a team captain.

I don't know who was more surprised – me or the producers of *A Question of Sport*. I would not have fancied being the games manufacturer who had brought out thousands of *A Question of Sport* games showing Bill Beaumont and Emlyn Hughes smiling out from the box lid. It was a startling poaching job that involved, as I understand it, highly secretive negotiations with Emlyn's agent Bev Walker.

There is no doubt that Hughes was a prize capture for Central, who had got him with the guarantee of a package deal of which *Sporting Triangles* was just a part. But I was left with a bitter taste in my mouth, not because Hughes had been signed but because I had been deliberately left in the dark about it. Gary Newbon had been taking me into his confidence for the previous eight years, but he chose not to give me a hint of what was going on. A lot of people saw the arrival of Hughes as a challenge to my standing at Central, but I honestly didn't give a damn. I would just like to have had knowledge of it before it was made public.

This was all a prelude to what was to be an almighty bust-up.

In the winter of 1989 I was in Birmingham for a meeting about what improvements we could make to *Sporting Triangles*. I was sitting in the Central canteen having my lunch after the meeting when producer Jeff Farmer came in looking sheepish. 'You'll never guess what Gary has gone and done,' he said. 'He's only agreed a deal that allows Emlyn to wear his own sponsored sweaters on the show.'

I chuckled. 'That will please the wardrobe department,' I said. 'Central spent fourteen hundred quid on new *Sporting*

Triangles sweaters at the start of the last series. Still, at least Andy and I can carry on wearing them.'

A few days later – with a week to go to the recording of the series – Jeff phoned me at home and told me that I didn't have to worry about which sweater to wear. 'We've just got a new stock in,' he said. 'They're red and look superb.'

Jeff is usually a real joker (except when the many horses that he backs don't get in the frame), but I detected from the tone of his voice that something was not quite right. And then the penny dropped.

'Jeff,' I said quietly and deliberately, 'these sweaters aren't by any chance Emlyn Hughes endorsed sweaters, are they?'

The silence on the other end of the line was deafening. 'Yes,' he finally admitted. 'But they don't have any distinguishing markings or logos on them.'

'I don't give a monkey's what they look like,' I said. 'There is no way in a million years that I will wear an Emlyn Hughes sweater.'

I could tell that Jeff was embarrassed, and I knew that he was just acting as a go-between for Gary Newbon.

'Have you got any red sweaters at home?' Jeff asked.

'Of course I have,' I said.

'All right, Jim. Wear one of your own. Just make sure it's red.'

Thirty minutes later the phone rang again. This time it was his high and mightiness Gary Newbon. We had a real slanging match that made the telephone wires sizzle.

'You *will* wear the sweater,' Newbon said in a threatening tone. 'If you don't you'll regret it. You will be sued for every penny you've got for breach of contract.'

'Where does it say in my contract that I've got to wear a sponsored sweater?' I said. 'There is no way that I'm going to wear it. You know where you can stick it.'

Our conversation ended with Gary slamming the telephone down on me. It stretched close to breaking point a friendship that had been good for most of the eight and a bit years that I had been with Central. I am the one who usually goes over the top when my temper soars, but this time there is no doubt at all that it was Gary who was right out of order. We barely spoke to each other over the next six months and you could have cut the atmosphere between us with a knife. And all over a bloody sweater.

Our row was the talk of Central, and inevitably the story was leaked to the press. I compounded it by giving the background details on TV-am, and then rubbed it in by saying on *Saint and Greavsie* that Emlyn Hughes was somebody who had proved that it *is* possible to fool all of the people all of the time. This enraged them at Central and Bob Southgate called my agent Barry Brown to warn me to lay off. In particular, they took exception to me continually calling the show *Snoring Triangles*. I had to admit that I was going in a bit strong. Hell hath no fury like an opinionator scorned!

Jeff Farmer came back on to me and said he had decided that I could wear which ever sweater I wanted. By then I felt I had made my point, and for the sake of Jeff's peace of mind I agreed to wear an Emlyn Hughes sweater.

It was all reported in the press as a punch-up between Hughes and myself, but the crazy thing is that Emlyn and I did not exchange a single word on the subject. In fact throughout the three weeks that it took to record the *Sporting Triangles* series we hardly had any sort of off-camera conversation apart from swapping brief pleasantries. My argument was not with Emlyn. It was over the principle of being ordered to wear an endorsed sweater. I feel sure he would have reacted the same if he had been told to wear a Jimmy Greaves endorsed sweater (Can I interest any maufacturers? I know where I can get them cheap from Taiwan!).

The only time I came close to reviving the dispute was in the green room after a recording of one of the *Sporting Triangles* shows. I accidentally found myself standing in the same company as Emlyn's agent Bev Walker, who smiled at me. I scowled back and gave him a verbal volley right between the eyes. I felt, rightly or wrongly, that he had played a prominent part in the Great Sweater Saga and I told him in no uncertain terms that I did not want him anywhere near me. My outburst made heads turn in the green room where I was suddenly seeing red.

O'Reilly was on the loose again!

I was convinced I was finished with Central, but after the third series of *Sporting Triangles* – the best so far thanks to the anchor work of Andy Craig and the input of giggly Emlyn – I got a telephone call from Barry Brown.

'Just listen and don't say a word until I've finished,' he said. 'I've been talking to Central about the next series of *Sporting*

Triangles. They want you and are prepared to pay for the privilege.'

Barry then told me what the fee would be. It was an offer I could not refuse. Sweater or no sweater.

There you go again, Greavsie. Selling your soul for a few pieces of silver. The good news is that I patched up my differences with garrulous Gary. He owed me an apology, but then I owe him gratitude for all he did to help me early in my television career. Perhaps I should buy him a present as a gesture of my gratitude. How about a sweater?

The sweater dispute has done no harm to Gary Newbon. Following the move of my former sparring partner John Bromley into the world of independents he has risen to heady heights as No 2 to his eminence Bob Burrows in the ITV sports hierarchy. In fact my old mate has become a high jumper.

While the sweater row was at its height I was saddened by the death of a good pal of mine – Dave Underwood, who as a goalkeeper gave sound service to QPR, Watford, Liverpool and Fulham. As my little personal tribute to a wonderful bloke I am going to relate one of my all-time favourite stories about the legendary Stanley Matthews.

Stanley and I were playing together in Kuwait for a 'golden oldies' team in the summer of 1972, the year after I had bowed out of League football. Sir Stanley was then 57 years young, and had been retired for seven years. It was the first time that I had played with him since having the privilege of partnering him in his farewell match at Stoke back in 1965 (a special bone china 'Stanley Matthews' tea service that was presented to each of the players that night remains one of my prized possessions).

Also in our team in Kuwait were players of the calibre of Johnny Haynes, John Charles, George Cohen, Ron Springett and the bearded wonder, Jimmy Hill. The temperature was a roasting 110 degrees Fahrenheit and most of us were knackered just by the walk from the dressing-room to the pitch. Stanley being Stanley, he refused to consider taking a breather and exhausted himself with a series of his twinkle-toed dribbles. It would never have entered proud Stanley's head to allow himself to be substituted, and when he saw our manager Dave Underwood waving for him to come off – with us losing 4–1 against the local Kuwait club – he immediately walked out of earshot and moved across to the left wing. Dave thought quickly and walked right the way around the perimeter of the pitch with the game in full flow and held up his arms as if parting the Red Sea. Dave then cupped his hands to his mouth and shouted at the top of his voice, 'Gentlemen, it is my privilege to accompany the great Sir Stanley Matthews off the pitch. Please accord him the ovation that he deserves.'

First of all the Kuwaiti players started to applaud, and then the capacity crowd took it up and cheered Stanley – escorted by Dave Underwood in almost a butlering role – as the Wizard of Dribble made a reluctant exit.

It was the only time in his life that he was substituted.

The relatively young Cliff Jones replaced the old master and, with his fresh legs, we pulled back to force a 4–4 draw.

This hilarious incident came to my mind along with a tear to my eye when I attended a special memorial service for Dave, who had passed on at the age of 60. It put into perspective my stupid row over a sweater.

Dave was a larger-than-life character with a nose flattened across his face like a heavyweight boxer. When the often eccentric Vic Buckingham was manager at Fulham he used to take Dave around with him and introduce him as, 'my chauffeur, Appleyard.'

Above all else Dave Underwood was a great human being who gave me his support in his days as Barnet chairman when I used to play for him while battling to beat the bottle.

I love the characters of football, and they don't come much greater than Dave Underwood. And certainly no greater than the man who features in my next chapter ... an astonishing bloke by the name of Brian Clough.

CHAPTER SEVEN

A call from Cloughie

My agent Barry Brown rang me during the 1988–89 football season as the reluctant go-between for a Fleet Street newspaper. 'I am duty bound to put the following offer to you,' he said. 'A Sunday newspaper (he named which one) is trying to stand up a story that Brian Clough has a drink problem. They say they know you've been talking to him and are willing to pay twenty-five thousand pounds for revealing what advice you gave him.'

'Tell them I don't know what they're on about,' I said.

Ten minutes later Barry rang back. 'They've upped the offer to thirty thousand,' he said.

'The answer is still no,' I said. 'As far as I'm aware, Cloughie does not have any problem. Tell them to lay off.'

I contacted his good pal Brian Moore to tell him to warn Cloughie that reporters were poking their noses into places where they did not belong. Mooro has had a long and close association with Cloughie, and I knew that he was genuinely concerned about the rumours that were scorching around the football world about Brian's drinking habits.

The reason I put on record the big-money bribe that was made to me is not to show what a goody two-shoes I was to turn it down but to illustrate the depth of interest there is in one of the most incredible characters British sport has ever produced. Cloughie was in the news at the time (when isn't he?) for thumping Nottingham Forest fans who had run onto the pitch. Around about the same time he had apparently made a bit of a twit of himself at the private wedding reception of a Scotsman when he allegedly put his hand up the groom's kilt. Fleet Street started putting two and two together, and the verdict was that he had become the puppet of alcohol.

What rubbish! Fleet Street reporters are wasting their time and energy trying to pin a scandal on Cloughie. There is no problem that the old master cannot handle, and to the best of my knowledge he drinks no more or less than any other manager. Anyway, Cloughie is big enough (and ugly enough) to fight his own battles, but I want to go on record as saying that what he does in his private life away from the football ground is nobody's business but his own.

Cloughie has not got a problem, but I do know that many managers turn to the bottle as a release valve from the pressures of management. This could be why the monthly Bell's Whisky Award for managers is so popular. Tommy Docherty, another marvellous character, once said: 'Managing a football club either drives you to drink or it drives you insane. I'll have a double please!'

One famous Football League manager was known as Champagne Charlie because of the amount of bubbly he used to get down his throat. There were only two people in the club who could drink more than him – his chairman and his centre-forward. The story goes that the manager was finally booted out, *not* because of his boozing but for bedding the wife of one of the directors. She picked up the bed-side telephone after they had finished their forty-five minutes each way, rang her husband and said: 'I'm in bed with your manager.'

It seems managers need an outlet for the pressures of their job, and if it is not the bottle then it's often the bed that gets them into trouble. Tommy Docherty, Malcolm Allison, John Bond, Harry Catterick, John Neal and Ron Atkinson are among those who have made bedtime story headlines. Their sexploits helped inspire a novel that I am hoping to have republished. It's called *The Boss* which is full of true stories that I have collected over the years about managers, but in which I have changed the names to protect the guilty. I will need to give it added spice for my fiction to keep pace with fact. How on earth can I match the sensational allegations that two red-heads – not one, but two – made about their bed-hopping fun and games with my old England team-mate Bobby Robson?

Come on you reds! It's a funny old game.

Getting back to Cloughie, I don't always agree with what he has to say in the context of football, but the game is richer for his presence. If he were to bow out of the game tomorrow he would be able to look back proudly at one of the greatest of all careers. I have personal reasons for having a special regard for him.It was the autumn of 1979 and I was just starting to put my life together again after my well-publicised nosedive into a sea of booze when I received an unexpected telephone call at home.

The voice in my ear belonged unmistakably to Brian Clough.

He said: 'Hey, young man, I just want you to know I'm here to give you any help I can. If you don't accept my offer of help I'll come down there and murder you. Got it?'

It was an offer I couldn't refuse. I told Cloughie that I was just starting out as a freelance journalist and he insisted: 'The moment you've settled to your new way of life, come to Nottingham and we'll have a long talk. You can publish the interview. No fee required.'

That's the sort of man Cloughie is behind his brash, and sometimes bombastic exterior. It's all a mask, really, hiding a caring man who sincerely wants to help others.

It was several months before I took him up on his offer of an interview, and while making preparations for this book I came across our tape-recorded conversation. I feel it is worth repeating here just to show what vision the man has. This is what we had to say to each other some ten years ago . . .

J G: 'Do you remember our first game together for England back in 1959?'

BC: 'Remember it? Hey, I can still feel it and taste it as though it were played yesterday. It was against Wales at Cardiff and the forward line was John Connelly, you and me, Bobby Charlton and my Middlesbrough colleague Edwin Holliday.'

J G: 'You and Holliday were both making your England debuts.'

BC: 'Correct. We were both Middlesbrough lads by birth but as different in temperament as it's possible to be. I was a bag of nerves and desperate to do well among all you household names, but Holliday seemed completely unconcerned by it all. I remember that he arrived without his boots and his mam brought them down by train and delivered them at the ground 25 minutes before the kick-off. That would have destroyed me, but Ed casually sat down and started changing the studs, whistling away as if he didn't have a care in the world. That was my introduction to the atmosphere of international football.'

J G: 'You were outspoken, Brian, even in those days.'

BC: 'You call it being outspoken. I call it having an opinion.'

J G: 'I remember you being worried about who was going to give you the ball.'

BC: 'Dead right, I was worried. There was I stuck in the middle of the two biggest names in football – yourself and the

Master, Robert Charlton – and I couldn't see who was going to pass to me. We were all receivers rather than givers. When I pointed this out to team manager Walter Winterbottom, he said: "Just go out there and inter-change and then go on and strike for goal." He made it sound as easy as putting jam on bread.'

J G: 'We drew 1–1 and Walter picked the same attack for the match against Sweden at Wembley 11 days later.'

B C: 'My second and last match for England. The mix was all wrong and I was the one who got the chop. Lost it 3–2. That result is carved into my heart. Something happened in that game that should have put me in the Guinness Book of Records. The ball hit the underside of the bar and I somehow managed to sit on it on the goal-line. It was trapped under my unmentionables and I couldn't move to put it in the net. I sat on it so long it's a wonder I didn't hatch the bloody thing!'

J G: 'Thinking back to when we were youngsters just coming into the game, we had some marvellous players to inspire us. I'm thinking of the likes of Matthews, Carter, Mannion, Lawton, Lofthouse, Finney, Shackleton. Where have all the great individual players gone?'

B C: 'It's much more of a team game now, young Jim. Coaching has had a lot to do with the disappearance of really creative players. Too many coaches are frightened of genius. They don't know how to handle it. So they take the easy way out and destroy it. I'm not against coaching but bad coaching is a criminal offence. It's a sad fact of life that there are more bad coaches than good ones, and they are the people who set out to destroy rather than create.'

J G: 'Who was your favourite of those glittering stars of our youth, and could he fit into today's football?'

B C: 'I would have to plump for Tom Finney. He was a real master and a marvellous ambassador for the game both on and off the pitch. I will always remember my first overnight stay with an England squad. We were in a posh hotel and I was a kid from the sticks, completely overawed by the surroundings and the big-name players.

'I was having a breakfast of bacon and baked beans and was so nervous that I tipped the lot on my lap. There are a lot of footballers who would have made capital of that and made my life a misery by taking the mickey. But that nice man Finney helped me clear myself up and quietly arranged for the hotel to clean my trousers.

'They were the only pair I had with me and I was so green that I didn't even realise you could get things cleaned and ironed in a hotel.'

J G: 'Footballers can be really cruel with the mickey taking. But Tommy's always been the first gentleman of the game.'

BC: 'I always stamp on anybody taking the mickey out of a club-mate. When Roger Davies first signed for Derby he had to take some unmerciful ribbings from established first-teamers. It got out of hand until I threatened that if anybody else took the mickey out of him I would give them a whack on the nose.

'Another time here at Forest, Garry Birtles was going through it because I kept beating him at squash. I put a notice on the board saying that anybody wanting to take the mickey out of Garry's ability on the squash court should challenge me for a £10 sidestake. The mickey taking stopped.'

J G: 'We've deviated a bit here, Brian. Can you talk a bit longer about Tom Finney?'

BC: 'A bit longer? I could talk all day about that man. He could play in any forward position. People seem to remember him best as a winger, but don't forget that in the later stages of his career he switched to centre-forward, and he was brilliant. Took all the knocks without complaint and tormented the hell out of defenders with sheer skill.

'If he were just starting in today's game he would have no trouble at all adjusting, simply because there's no substitute for skill.'

J G: 'There are not many skilful youngsters coming through in the game today. Are you concerned about the lack of talent?'

BC: 'Hey, Jim, the trouble with you is since you switched to this writing and broadcasting lark you've joined the army of pessimists. Let me tell you that English football is like a diamond mine. There are lots of shining talents around. They need cutting and polishing and putting in the right setting, but if you look after them properly they will dazzle. The game is in a healthy state despite what the obituary writers might say. We can all go forward together with confidence about the future provided a few attitudes are changed.'

J G: 'What is needed to lift our football out of its present slump?'

BC: 'There's an easy answer. A successful England team. Ron Greenwood carries a lot of responsibility. He's got to get a team together that will get us through to the 1982 World Cup finals and then we need to do well in Spain. If we shine in Spain it will reflect in our attendances at home.'

JG: 'Are you optimistic of our chances of making a strong challenge for the World Cup?'

BC: 'Provided Ron picks our best team, yes.'

JG: 'That sounds an odd thing to say.'

BC: 'Well let me tell you, young man, that while I may have a reputation for shooting my mouth off you would be amazed at the amount of listening I've done over the years. Two men I listened to more than most were Harry Storer and Bill Shankly and they both gave me the same advice: "Always select your best team." That statement will no doubt baffle the laymen but you would be surprised how many managers don't, for various reason, pick the best possible team that is available to them.'

JG: 'Have we got the players to make us a world power?'

BC: 'Without question. There are plenty of those diamonds I was telling you about in our game. It's up to the England manager to pick them and make them dazzle. It might hurt old pros like you and me to hear this said, Jim, but many of today's players are technically better than in our day. Better than me anyway, but you, of course, were a genius. And make sure you leave that on tape for your readers.'

JG: 'Changing the subject quickly, do you go along with the growing belief that players are now taking too much money out of the game?'

BC: 'Football is just beginning to stabilise after the introduction of freedom of contract. At first players went berserk asking for fortunes and managers and clubs went equally mad by agreeing to give them what they were demanding.'

JG: 'And you think it's now under control?'

BC: 'I wouldn't go as far as saying that, but we at least now know what's to be done. Footballers must be made to understand the facts of life otherwise they will be putting clubs out of business. They will have to understand that if there's £20,000 coming in, they can only have £19,000 between them. If they take £21,000 that's bad business for their club and ultimately bad business for them because at that rate the club wouldn't be there for longl I think we are coming into a period in our game where common sense will prevail and greed will take a back seat.'

JG: 'It's good to hear you in a buoyant, optimistic mood.'

BC: 'Why shouldn't I be? When you look around here at the Forest ground with its new £2.5-million stand and the trophies that the club have won in the last few years you have to be optimistic about what can be achieved in football. If Forest can do this, then there's hope for all clubs. We're only a little club y'know, but it's not stopped us thinking and acting big. That's the art of management. Taking decisions and putting your head on the chopping block for them. You're soon found out in this game if you try to do anything by halves. You can't hide. Every decision is there to be judged. Many clubs can have our sort of success provided they get their management right. That may sound conceited but it's an honest opinion. I'm always getting myself into hot water by speaking my mind but our football might be in a better state if more people were more honest and direct with their opinions.'

JG: 'Do you think there's less honesty in the game these days?'

BC: 'Let's say there's less sincerity. I look around the board-rooms and I see more sharks than there used to be. They are coming into the game for the wrong reasons, buying their way into clubs for image and appearances sake rather than because they have a genuine love for football. Some of the dignity is going out of the game and I think that's sad.'

JG: 'What advice would you give any young manager coming into the game?'

BC: 'Be creative. Don't wear blinkers. Have opinions and really MANAGE.'

JG: 'If you were running our game, Brian, what changes would you introduce to improve it and make its future more secure?'

BC: 'For a start, I would put you out of work with your ATV job. I would ban television cameras from all grounds for a period of three years. A total blackout. There is no question in my mind that television is doing untold damage to our game. The weekend before last I saw highlights and goals from nine FA Cup matches. Why should anybody bother to leave their armchairs when they know they can enjoy a bonanza on their television screens?'

JG: 'But surely football needs the money from TV fees?'

BC: 'We've sold it too cheap and it's costing the major clubs money in possible shirt sponsorship income. I want to see football banned from the TV screens for three years during which we in the game must work at getting people back into the habit of going to the grounds to see football in the flesh. Then after the three-year ban, I would sit down with TV bosses and negotiate a sensible deal that would allow just one live 90-minute match to be shown, possibly on a Sunday afternoon. I don't like the filleted service that we get at the moment, with edited matches in which only goals and controversial incidents are shown. Let's have just one game, warts an' all.'

JG: 'I don't think your blanket ban would be popular with senior citizens and invalids who rely on their television sets for their football entertainment.'

BC: 'They have my deepest sympathy and I would think proposals could be made to make entrance fees as cheap as possible for senior citizens. My heart bleeds for the people unable to leave their homes, but to be brutally honest our game will become a sick invalid unless we stop television luring so many of our customers away.'

JG: 'You mentioned possible live coverage of a match on a Sunday afternoon. Are you in favour of Sunday football?'

BC: 'Deep down, no. My missus says she'll walk out on me if regular Sunday football comes. It's the only day that sanity comes to our household and we can lead a normal, family life. That's important to me. But I won't fight against Sunday football if it is proved that this is what the public wants. I just won't campaign for it. Ideally I would like to see Sunday Summer afternoon football watched by families in shirt sleeves and colourful summer dresses. That would be Utopia. But then what would happen to our family get-togethers at home and what would happen to Sunday cricket? As you can see, Jim, I'm fairly torn apart on the subject of Sunday football. It will be the public that decides whether it is to become a regular fixture.'

JG: 'If you could make one law change to make football a better spectacle, what would it be?'

BC: 'I don't think the laws need to be tampered with to any great degree. One thing I would like to see is for any offence in the penalty area to be punished with a penalty. Obstruction, dangerous kicking, spitting, any misconduct. Make it a penalty. Those free-kicks in the box are a farce.'

J G: 'Imagine that it's 1990. How do you see the game being played and presented?'

B C: 'I don't think there will be that much difference in the way the game is played but there will be a big change in the presentation. There will be a lot more razzmatazz with clubs going all out to attract family audiences. I hope there will be a lot of all-seater stadiums and that hooliganism will be just a bad memory.'

J G: 'What will Brian Clough be doing in 1990?'

B C: 'I think you and I will be pushing each other around in wheelchairs, Jim. I just can't visualise that I will still be in management. The generation gap between me and the players would be too wide. I can still put them in their place at the moment by taking them on to the squash court and beating them. But I think that will be beyond me when I'm 55. Some cocky little 18-year-old will be able to say: "Look at that silly old bastard!" I will have lost the gift of communication that's so important between a manager and his players. I can't have them calling me "Grandad".'

J G: 'Well I think you will still need football, Brian. And football will definitely need you. If I were running football in this country I know that by 1990 I would have you well established in the England manager's chair.'

That was how we wound up our taped conversation, and listening to it ten years on I am saddened and angered that Cloughie was never given the England manager's job. It should have been his when Don Revie deserted, but the chicken-hearted men who run our game did not have the courage to appoint him and played it safe by giving the job to 'Reverend' Ron Greenwood. I spent my final dismal season under Greenwood's management at West Ham, and I can state with some knowledge that he was not in the same league as Cloughie. He talked a good game, but was too much of a theorist. Ron used to go over the heads of many of his players with his tactical talks, and did not have the powers of motivation that are so vital to a manager. Cloughie is Churchillian in the way he can inspire a team by saying the right thing at the right time.

People tend to forget that the spell that Cloughie has been weaving at Nottingham Forest is nothing new to that corner of England. He was performing similar wonders just fifteen miles away at Derby until sensationally resigning in 1973 with his team lying third in the First Division.

Dynamic, driving, single-minded, perceptive, inspiring, controversial, stubborn, ruthless, courageous, energetic, tough, ambitious, egotistical – all these ingredients have gone into the cocktail character that, shaken not stirred, makes Cloughie one of the most successful managers of all time. There is no question that he would be the people's popular choice as manager of England, but the establishment have always feared him as being too hot to handle.

Beneath the skin of the tough, uncompromising manager is a sensitive and loving family man (who in son, Nigel, has produced one of the most talented British footballers of modern times). Brian is immensely proud of his profession and a quiet fighter for good causes. It's fitting that he is building his legend in Robin Hood's Nottingham territory. I get the feeling that in another age Cloughie would willingly have robbed the rich to help the poor. He is continually doing charitable work without seeking publicity, and I know better than most that when you are in trouble he is ready to help without seeking anything in return.

I make no apologies for devoting a chapter to Cloughie. It gives me the chance to make public my gratitude for the kindness he showed me when I had that bad hiccup in my life.

It is one of the football crimes of the century that he was never given command of the England team. His decisive attitude could have sent a breath of fresh air right through our game, but the establishment has always been frightened of his magnetic attraction for controversy.

I suppose it's a case of history repeating itself. Robin Hood hardly endeared himself to the establishment!

I have cocked a deaf ear to the rumours about Cloughie and the booze because, as I am about to reveal, I have had plenty of painful experience of how wickedly wrong gossip-spreading witnesses can be.

CHAPTER EIGHT

Mistaken identity

'Greavsie's back on the booze and rampaging through Birmingham!'

This was the story that shot round the Midlands at about the time that I was having my bad-tempered quarrels with Roy Bottomley. It was pure fiction, but several newspapers were trying to turn it into fact.

I had got wind that something was up when Olivia, Gary Newbon's secretary at Central, telephoned me at home.

'Are you all right?' she asked, sounding almost nervous.

'As right as I'll ever be. Why, what's the matter?'

'There are rumours everywhere up here that you're back on the bottle,' she said, 'I knew it was nonsense, but I thought I should warn you that a newspaper has been on to the Press office asking questions. They've had a tip-off that you are drinking again.'

'Let them go ahead and print it,' I said. 'It will be like money in the bank for me.

Then I was confronted by a freelance, who said he had spoken to half a dozen independent witnesses who claimed they had seen me involved in drunken incidents in Birmingham. They reported seeing me legless and swearing at the top of my voice during a brawl in a hotel bar with the producer of my chat show, and I had also allegedly smashed up a hotel bedroom, been thrown out of a pub and had been involved in a punch-up with passers-by in the street.

I admitted to a slight altercation with Roy Bottomley, but explained that it was nothing approaching a drunken brawl. 'It was bottles of Perrier water at six paces,' I said. 'I'll own up to having put my tongue to a few choice words, but that's the only true fact in the entire story.'

It was only after I had managed to convince the reporter that I had been in Cornwall on the days of the other alleged incidents that he realised with undisguised disappointment that he had got the wrong man.

A few days later I read a story that actor Michael Elphick – star of the hit Central series *Boon* – had been raging through Birmingham on the sort of drunken binge that had once been my speciality. The report, so I thought, cleared up the mystery as to why I had been the subject of such close scrutiny. 'Elphick is a Jimmy Greaves look-alike,' I read. 'This led to reports that Greavsie was back on the booze, but Jimmy laughed off the rumours. He said, 'I know lots of things are happening in my life at the moment, but the last thing I need to do is start drinking again.'

Then a few days later I discovered that the report about Michael Elphick was also wrong. He admitted to having a problem with booze, but strenuously denied that he was the man bingeing through Birmingham.

It was also reported that I had been helping Michael combat his problem. The truth of it is that I was asked by a Central colleague if I could have a quiet word with Michael, but by then he had checked himself into a clinic and was being sensible enough to tackle the problem himself without having me poking my nose into his private affairs. He had the character to beat the bottle, and it was great to see him back as *Boon* looking clear eyed, trim and alert.

It amused me that half of Birmingham seemed to think that I was back on the bottle. It was a classic case of mistaken identity. My only regret is that I did not keep my trap shut and allow the stories to be printed about my alleged return to the booze. The way the high courts have been dishing out the dosh in libel cases I could have been on to a nice little earner.

There have been literally dozens of occasions when people have thought I was back on the booze. My quick temper has helped to fuel the rumours, and it is common for my closest friends to receive hush-hush calls from reporters along the lines of 'We've had a tip-off that Greavsie is back on the bottle. Have you been doing anything to help him beat it?'

The Saint got such a call in the autumn of 1988 after I had cancelled all off-screen engagements for a month. A shocking cold had left me with a throat that was as sore as if I had been cleaning it with a wire brush. Somebody tipped off a newspaper that I had pulled out of all my work because I was drinking.

'I think the old boy's just getting on in life,' the Saint told the reporter, shooting down in flames his Greavsie's-back-on-the-booze line. 'I don't know anything other than he's had a very bad throat and feels in need of a rest. He had the same problem last year.'

This did not stop the newspaper running a story full of innuendo, referring to my past drinking exploits and headlined, RIDDLE AS GREAVSIE GOES MISSING. I was missing to such an extent that I could be seen every Monday morning sitting on the couch at TV-am who had invited me back to join my favourite team following my 'holiday' in Cornwall. Perhaps the reporter thought that it was my *Spitting Image* dummy who was previewing the week's television. Sometimes it's hard to tell the difference.

Regularly every year I have a throat and chest problem. The crazy thing is that I have more illnesses now than I ever used to when I was hitting the bottle. The alcohol might have been making a mess of my liver, but on the way it was killing off a lot of germs.

Another Greavsie's-back-on-the-bottle rumour started when I pulled out of the *Big Match Live* team in 1988. 'Is it true that Jimmy drinks at weekends and that is why he prefers to keep out of the public spotlight?' one reporter asked a colleague of mine. The prat.

I kicked the *Big Match* job into touch simply because I was overdoing it. My crazy weekend schedule was:

TV-am at Camden on Friday morning
Central TV at Birmingham on Friday evening
LWT for the *Saint and Greavsie* show on Saturday
Manchester (for instance) for the *Big Match* on Sunday
TV-am at Camden on Monday morning

This left me no time to breathe, let alone get stuck into the booze. Yes, I was making a good living. But who wants to be the richest corpse in the cemetery?

I have got news for all those people who have been reporting me as being back on the booze: **I have not touched a drop of alcohol since 28th February, 1978.**

I can be specific about the date and even the place where I had my last drop. It was eight days after my thirty-eighth birthday and I had been on an almighty bender that ended with me being taken into a ward for the mentally disturbed at Warley Hospital in Essex. Fleet Street were on to the story, and on the Saturday evening before my shame was to be spread across the

Sunday front pages I walked out of Warley Hospital and called in at the White Horse in Brentwood, which was the nearest pub. It was after 10 o'clock in the evening and the place was packed. I had to almost battle my way to the bar where I ordered a pint of best bitter and knocked it back without it touching the sides of my throat. It was a wonder I had any room for the liquid because over the previous fortnight I had drunk myself into a stupor. Yet I still had a raging thirst and, with just minutes to closing time, I ordered a second pint and that went down just as quickly.

The barman called 'Last Orders' and I started to push my way back towards the bar. I was jostled this way and that, and suddenly I said, 'Oh bollocks to it.' With that I walked out of the pub and away from boozing. I knew that from the moment the newspapers hit the doormats the next morning I would be on show, and I was determined to prove that I could beat it. Not once since then has a drop of alcohol passed my lips.

To this day I still consider myself an alcoholic. Once an alcoholic, always an alcoholic. But today I am sober.

While I am on the theme of boozing, I would like to take this opportunity to pay respects to the memory of one of my old drinking pals who was my favourite boardroom character: John Cobbold, the former chairman of Ipswich Town who has now passed on to the big brewery in the sky. Known to everybody in Ipswich as 'Mister John,' he was one of the great English eccentrics, a marvellously warm and affectionate man with a heart as big as his head.

I had many happy hours in Mister John's company in the days when we used to try to drink each other under the table. These are just a few of the stories I collected from him during our days of wine and roses....

Returing from a skiing holiday, Mister John was nicely under the influence when he got off the train at Ipswich. He felt that the train driver deserved reward for getting him home safely and so gave him his skis! 'Well,' said Mister John, 'you tip a taxi-driver. Why not a train-driver?'

Jackie Milburn – another late, great hero of mine – was deeply concerned about a losing sequence when he was manager at Ipswich. He buttonholed the chairman during a train journey from Liverpool Street to Ipswich. He talked long and passionately about where he felt things were going wrong, and what could be done to put things right. Jackie was just building up to telling the chairman that he would need some money to spend in the transfer market, and felt the moment was right because he was convinced he had Mister John's total attention. He was about to quote the price for a player when the chairman pointed out of the train window and exclaimed, 'Just look at the size of the bollocks on that bull . . .'

Alf Ramsey was close to Cobbold during his days as a phenomenally successful manager at Ipswich. They could not have been more opposite in personality and background. Mister John might have stepped out of the pages of a P. G. Wodehouse Bertie Wooster story. He was a fun-loving Old Etonian brewery owner from the privileged classes whose uncle was the governor of the Bank of England. Alf, from Dagenham, was more *Roy of the Rovers* material. He had been born on a tiny smallholding, the son of a hay and straw dealer, and he had left school at fourteen. While Mister John was outgoing and extrovert, Alf could be brooding and as expressionless as a stone Sphinx. Yet despite all their differences there was a tremendous rapport between the two men, and Mister John gave Alf many lessons in how to exercise his elbow; in return, Alf tried to teach his chairman the finer points of football.

'Everybody thought Alf was unemotional, but he just hid his feelings, that's all,' said Mister John. 'When we won the League championship in 1962 Alf waited until everybody but me had left the ground. Then he told me to go and sit in the directors box. When I sat myself down I saw through an alcoholic fog Alf doing a lone lap of honour around the pitch and in front of empty terraces.'

Ipswich were involved in a relegation battle during one particular season and Mister John was asked what he was going to do about the crisis. 'Crisis?' said Mister John. 'What crisis? My dear boy, what we consider a crisis here is when we run out of whisky in the boardroom. *That's* a crisis.'

Once when Ipswich had landed a big sponsorship contract, Mister John said at the Press launch, 'It has been unfairly suggested that we will squander the sponsors' money on wine, women and song. That is absolute nonsense. We don't do much singing at Ipswich . . .!'

John Cobbold. A real one-off. I was just thinking that there were no more personalities in the boardroom when who should explode on to the scene but Michael Knighton, suddenly

The family man. Here are the Greavsies on parade for Lynn's wedding in 1980. From left to right: Danny, Mitzi, the old man, Lynn, the love of my life Irene and young Andy.

I'm on 'giving away' duty again in 1981 with our second daughter, Mitzi.

Showing that Dad's still boss with the ball in a kickabout with football-daft Danny and Andy.

The media man! This is me in my new world of television – on the studio floor at Central.

With my faithful clipboard.

At the start of my TV career on 'Star Soccer'.

This is my old sparring partner Gary Newbon (left) and a racing camel (right) after I had just beaten Bob Champion by a nostril in a charity race. Gary, as ever, is more interested in the camera than me or the camel. Only joking, pal.

Opposite top: With Britt Eckland.

Opposite below: Glamorous women were for ever popping in on my new chat show, but they never stayed to do the washing up! (Above) with Nina Carter (left) and Kate Robbins (right).

I'm on the ball for a publicity photograph to launch a new series of the 'On The Ball' programme when I first started my partnership with the Saint.

A great double-act.

Above: Saint gets his paws on the FA Cup.

Left: Big Frank tries to knock some sense into us.

V-neck sweaters all round . . . It must be 'Sporting Triangles'. Top, With Eric Bristow.

Below: With Nigel Benn.

announcing to a startled football world in the summer of 1989 that he was buying Manchester United for £20 million.

He declared that he was the shy, retiring type and then in the most extrovert act I have ever seen from a chairman did a ball juggling act in front of the Stretford End fans before United's first match of the 1989–90 season. He was showing off the skills he had perfected as an apprentice professional with Coventry City before injury ended his career. He then announced that he was ready to meet any League chairman in a ball-juggling contest for a £5 million bet, the money going to charity. This got me thinking, and I replied to his challenge with this article ordered by *The Sun* Sports Editor David Balmforth:

"I am today ready to accept Manchester United boss Michael Knighton's £5 million challenge to a ball-juggling contest. If I win the money will go to my favourite charity – Southend United Football Club.

'Hold on, Greavsie,' I can hear Knighton saying, 'my challenge is to League club chairmen.

Correct, and I want you to meet Chairman Jim!

I have asked my pal Vic Jobson, chairman at Southend, if I can take over his seat on the board at Roots Hall. I will stay in the chair for as long as it takes me to meet (and beat) moneybags Knighton in a juggling duel.

And here's a proposition for you, Michael. After we have seen who can keep our balls up longest, we shall meet in a double or quits penalty shoot out. Five shots each, and you can put United 'keeper Jim Leighton in goal. I always fancy myself to beat Jock goalkeepers. I'll bring Pat Jennings out of retirement to represent me in goal.

So the challenge now becomes a £10-million gamble.

I want a neutral referee to make sure that Knighton sticks to the rules. I don't want him shoving a wig on United director Bobby Charlton and sending him out as a ringer.

And I don't want him bringing his mate Rod Hull and that 'orrible Emu of his anywhere near the ground. If Emu were to try to grab my unmentionables I would send him gift-wrapped to Bernard Matthews.

For years I have been trying to work out how I could legally get my hands on a million smackers. I considered challenging

Mike Tyson, but now Michael Knighton has presented me with an easier way of earning it.

I will collect a modest ten per cent of the £10-million kitty. The rest would go to Southend United to help with their ambitious plans for a super new stadium. We could stage the contest in a ring raised in the middle of the Old Trafford pitch. I would make my entrance to the 'Eye of the Tiger' Rocky music. The obvious entrance music for Knighton would be, 'Chairman of the Board.' After we have finished the juggling jamboree, the ring will be dismantled and then it will be time for the penalty shoot out in a double or quits battle for ten million quid.

I can get plenty of backers for the match with Knighton. If I were to win and he could not put his hands on the readies because of all his commitments at Old Trafford I will happily take a couple of United players in lieu.

Southend manager David Webb (who once headed an FA Cup winning goal for Chelsea at Old Trafford) fancies Bryan Robson and Mark Hughes.

I am a closet Southend supporter and watch as many of their home matches as possible. They are always entertaining to watch (well they give me a good laugh any way). Some thirty-odd years ago I used to play with Vic Jobson in an Essex youth team that his dad helped run. He is pretty good at keeping a lot of balls in the air, but he agrees that I would have a better chance of outjuggling Knighton.

So now I wait to hear from United's shining knight.

What about it, Michael? Do you accept my counter challenge for £10 million pounds – winner takes all?

If the answer is 'yes' I shall attend the next Southend United board meeting to seek the official go ahead to take over as temporary chairman.

Whatever your decision, I would like to welcome you to the mad, mad, mad world of football. You have brought a much-needed sense of fun back into the game, and I hope it spreads to the pitch.

What we need is more ball jugglers. We must encourage the individualists back into game.

If a chairman can juggle his balls, why not the players?”

It was all good tongue-in-cheek fun, and Michael Knighton quickly picked up on it, and accepted my challenge. But then he did less well with his financial juggling, and after a month of wheeling and dealing he dropped his bid and instead settled for a compromise role as a director at Old Trafford.

If he ever makes it to the chair I shall be waiting to meet him in a juggling duel. At least for a short while Michael Knighton had brought some fun back into a game that is in desperate need of the kick of life.

CHAPTER NINE

The game I loved

What have they gone and done to the game that I loved? Football is not half the fun it used to be, and the skill and the splendour has been squeezed out of it like juice from an orange. Where there was once joy on the terraces there is now too often violence, and where there was once freedom of thought on the pitch there is now too often fear. Where there was once sense in the boardroom there is now too often insanity and selfishness, and where there was once loyalty in the players there is now galloping greed.

I have watched helpless from the sidelines the gradual decline and fall of our national game, and I have grown disillusioned as I've witnessed kick-and-rush teams like Wimbledon applauded for murdering our football, players like Vinny Jones lauded for their thug tactics, and loud-mouthed managers becoming bigger heroes than their players.

Our football is at the crisis crossroads as we come into the 1990s and we must set goals now if the game as we know it is still to be alive and kicking when the twenty-first century arrives.

I am getting these thoughts down on to paper in the awful wake of Hillsborough. If there is not a concerted effort to stop the downward spiral in our game then the click, click, click of the turnstiles will become the tick, tick, tick of a time-bomb that will blow our games to bits.

At this very moment there is a small clique of powerful men preparing to hijack our football and force on us a 'Super League' in which only a select handful of up to sixteen clubs will be involved (and, as I understand it, the elite squad could include Rangers and Celtic).

It will be great for the chosen few, but the vast majority of clubs will be left on the outside struggling for existence. We have now reached the stage where football has one last chance to get its act together, or the curtain will come down for all but the wealthiest clubs.

The only way to save our soccer is for everybody in the game – and I do mean everybody – to act immediately. There could be no better memorial to the 95 supporters who lost their lives in Sheffield than that we use the tragedy to turn our game into something of which we can be proud. At the moment the feeling is more one of shame and revulsion.

In my view (in advance of Lord Justice Taylor's report) the major points that should be top of any Save-Our-Soccer agenda are:

□GROUNDS. No club should be allowed to open its doors to fans unless it can guarantee safety and comfort. Within two years every club in the League must have, at the very least, 80 percent seating facilities. It is more than 50 years since a major football stadium was built in England. Wembley, despite all the money that has been spent dressing it up, belongs to yesterday's world. A new national stadium should – in fairness to all fans – be built in the heart of the country. Birmingham is the obvious place for the site. It is central, and there is space close to the National Exhibition Centre to build an all-seater stadium of which we can be proud, and with facilities suited to the twenty-first century.

□FINANCE. All the money that the Government takes in tax from the football pools companies over the next three years should be channelled into a grounds-improvement scheme. Every penny that the League takes from television should go into a central fund for the exclusive use of ground improvements.

□TRANSFERS. There should be an immediate freeze on major transfers until the ground improvements have been carried out. For the next two years no club should be allowed to spend more than £250,000 in any transfer transaction. I was horrified by the sale of Chris Waddle to Marseilles for more than four million pounds. Tottenham were right to take it. It was an offer they could not refuse. But there is now the Waddle factor in all transfer dealings. As good a player as Chris is, there is no way he is worth that sort of money. But suddenly players are measured by the value of Waddle, and all common sense has been shelved.

□HOOLIGANS. Magistrates must come down much more

heavily on any louts found guilty of causing problems inside or outside football grounds. Hooliganism is the real cancer in our game, and it must be cut out. There is only one place for young thugs who terrorise innocent people, and that is behind bars. If more hooligans were imprisoned then it would be a deterrent to other young louts who merely ape their elders. It is a problem as much of society as of soccer, and football clubs cannot bear it on their own. It is time for the big stick. There is a generation of kids growing up who have never been to a football match in their lives because parents, understandably, will not allow them anywhere near a football ground. Everything must be done to encourage family participation at football clubs, otherwise there will be no spectators to watch future games. It is when kids are at their most impressionable age that they get an allegiance to a club that lasts a lifetime. But many of today's youngsters have not seen in-the-flesh football and will have only a passing interest (no pun intended) in the game when they grow up.

□PLAYERS. I have been shown contracts of First and Second Division players that make my mind reel. Too many are making greedy demands and are not putting enough back into the game. There should be a two-year freeze on footballers' wages until the grounds are as they should be. I would also like to see a return to club loyalty among players. So many players jump on the transfer roundabout when their contracts are up that it's a wonder managers – let alone spectators – can recognise their team. As Tommy Docherty says, 'At the end of team talks today managers finish with "Good luck . . . whoever you are."' Players must recognise their responsibility to the public. Spectators are paying good money to watch them play, and are entitled to 100 per cent effort in return. And just a little personal advice from somebody who knows – lay off the booze. From the tales I am told, today's players make the footballers from my era seem like novices when it comes to drinking. It's just not worth it. One day you will not only wake up with a hangover, but also a problem that you cannot control.

□MANAGERS. For a start, they must accept that it is the *players* who should be getting the publicity, not them. I have yet to meet the spectator who goes to a match to watch the manager. Most of all, they must encourage freedom of expression on the pitch. Too many players have had any natural ability coached out of them by blinkered coaches. I shudder when I see the sort of big-boot football produced in recent seasons by the likes of Wimbledon, Millwall, Leeds, Sheffield Wednesday and Portsmouth. They should be prosecuted for cruelty to footballs. When I was a kid I could reel off the names of the players in my favourite teams, but I never used to have a clue who the managers were. Now fans can name the manager of their club, but few of the players that they pay to watch.

□REFEREES. Surely the time has come to have full-time professional referees whom the players can respect, instead of the jokers in black who turn matches into whistle-stop bores. It would make sense to encourage players to take refereeing courses so that they have a career to turn to when they hang up their boots.

□SPECTATORS. In return for not being treated like cattle, they must behave in an adult and dignified manner (as most of them do). Jostling and pushing on the way to and from grounds is not only idiotic but dangerous. A golden rule: Keep off the pitch at all times.

□CHAIRMEN. The most powerful men in the game must use all possible resources to improve their grounds, or get the backing of local councils for moves to areas where they can build stadiums suitable for football in the twenty-first century. If any chairman wrings his hands and says it can't be done, he should move over and let in the army of bright, imaginative young businessmen itching to become involved in a much-needed boardroom revolution.

□TELEVISION. The people who run football have still not learned how to use the power of television to give the game maximum exposure. When it comes to press and public relations, they are still living in the Ice Age. They are now collecting serious money for live matches, but the host clubs still do not open themselves up enough to encourage greater interest from the viewers that just might lead to them getting off their backsides and going to the ground. They adopt a take-it-or-leave-it attitude instead of seizing the chance to 'sell' their club to the millions of spectators watching from home. They should welcome the cameras to a behind-the-scenes view that will make the programme more interesting and, consequently, present their club in a better light. But no, the majority of clubs give only as much co-operation as they need to without thinking of how it would help them and the game to give the viewers a more intimate view of what goes on off the pitch.

I went to Italy to see my old club AC Milan play Real Madrid in the European Cup semi-final at the council-owned San Siro Stadium in 1989, and I have to report that we are light years behind in the football we play and in the facilities that we offer fans.

It hurts me to say it, but I think English clubs are even trailing the Jocks now; and there is no question that clubs like Rangers, Celtic and Aberdeen can show us how a modern football ground should look. Even unheralded St Johnstone are building a brand new stadium that will put England's Victorian age dumps to shame.

We must quickly get our football sorted out – on and off the pitch – if the quick-step towards the twenty-first century is not to become a funeral march for our once-proud game.

Out of the horror of Hillsborough let us find hope. We owe that much to the memory of 95 people whose lives were wasted.

The alternative will be the breakaway super league, which will mean all our traditions going out of the window. It will be good for a small minority, but football should not be for the elite. It is the game of the people, and a super league will mean that the majority of clubs will not get a look in.

That is how our football will be in the year 2000 unless action is taken NOW.

As this is a chapter devoted entirely to football I want to take the opportunity to stretch my thoughts to examine just what is going wrong with a game that has been so good to me in the past. I have seen the theory advanced that it has become too hard, but that is just nonsense. Anybody who says that has not had his shins autographed by the likes of Norman 'Bites Yer Legs' Hunter, Tommy 'The Anfield Iron' Smith or Ron 'Chopper' Harris. Vinny Jones would not have lived with them, but a major difference was that they could play football as well as put the boot in.

I promise you that the modern game is soft in comparison

with the 'sixties when football was under the rule of the boot. So why are there more sendings off than in my time?

One cause is the rise in sneaky and spiteful off-the-ball fouls such as elbows in the face and tapped ankles. They were what we used to call 'Continental fouls.' It is not hard play as understood by those who lived through the tough-but-honest Hunter-Smith-Harris-Mackay-Storey-Setters-Stiles era.

In my opinion (and I have the scars to prove I am entitled to comment) the main reason the game is getting beyond the control of referees is not that it is too hard, but because it is too *fast*.

The game has become so quick that referees just cannot keep up with it. They have become hurried with their decisions, and discretion and diplomacy seem to have been kicked well and truly into touch. It's almost as if they are being so quick on the draw with their cards because they want to buy time to catch their breath.

Perhaps the time has come for another experiment with the two-referee system. This was last tried back in the 1930s and was a failure, but that was in the days when football was played at a more sedate and sane pace. It just might be worth another experiment before our game gets totally beyond the control of the referees. Either that or give linesmen greater powers. Too often they seem to be like the three monkeys – seeing, hearing and saying nothing.

How often do you see linesmen in a position where they must have seen exactly what happened but are not asked for any sort of an opinion by the referee?

The quicker the referees, managers and players get round a table and talk openly about each other's problems the better it will be for what is suddenly not quite such a funny old game. Let's have jaw-jaw, not war-war!

We have switched from thinking football to a sprinting game. The reason a player like John Barnes gets so much deserved praise for his performances with Liverpool is that he is one of the few players still finding time to dwell on the ball and able to make his skill do the talking. Football has become a helter-skelter game for greyhounds. Players are dashing around at such a furious pace that they don't have time to think how they could use half the energy to achieve twice as much. They get rid of the ball so quickly now that you would think it was a bomb about to blow up in their face.

I believe that the blame for this thoughtless, reckless football lies at the feet of the coaches. They are slowly but surely squeezing the individualists out of our game. Hand on heart, how many players in the League would you go out of your way to watch because of their special skill and flair? I doubt if you could name more than half a dozen.

The reason is not that players are necessarily less talented than in the past. It is simply that they are not getting the right encouragement to flourish their skill. If the likes of great solo artists like Stanley Matthews, George Best and Len Shackleton were playing today they would be in trouble with coaches for hogging the ball.

What makes me feel quite ill is that Shackleton, the Clown Prince of Soccer who was my idol when I was a kid, won just five England caps. There are players now who have won ten times more caps than Shack yet do not have a tenth of his ability. They do not even belong on the same planet as him when it comes to skill, invention and flair. Shack could stop a game dead just by putting his foot on the ball, and he would dictate the pace and pattern of play with immaculate ball control and precise passing. When did you last see a player put his foot on the ball and actually think about where he was going to place it? He would get shot by today's coaches for stopping the flow of the game. Most of all, Shack was a character who saw the pitch as a stage and was always entertaining every time he stepped on it. Paul Gascoigne, from the North-East like Shack, is one of the rare 'personality' players in the game today, and he is also one of the few with the old-style skill to be able to conduct and control a match in his own time. Gazza does not chase around like a headless chicken.

I have a lot of good friends in the game who I know will disagree with my verdict that football has become too fast and frenzied. But they are too close to it. I am sure they would share my opinion if they could take the view that I am getting from the sidelines.

Our game will run deeper into trouble unless there is a big shift back towards the skill factor and an end to the running-wild stuff that passes for football.

My simple plea to the coaches is: *Give the game back to the players.*

Bob Paisley, football's elder statesman, tossed a hand-grenade into the world of soccer with the comment that the general standard of play in the First Division is the lowest it has ever been. I fully agreed with his observation, but I did not feel that 'Uncle' Bob showed his usual tact in making his opinion so public. It was the right sentiment out of the wrong mouth. Still a valued consultant at Anfield, he somehow managed to devalue the achievements of Kenny Dalglish's Liverpool team. They would come third on my list of great clubs sides of my lifetime. Here, for argument's sake, is my top ten table of post-war League championship-winning teams and the players representing them (I have selected only one team for each club, which means, for instance, that Manchester United's 1968 European Cup winning team is pipped by the Busby Babes of 1956–57):

1. **Manchester United** (1956–57)
   Wood, Foulkes, Byrne, Colman, Jones, Edwards, Berry, Whelan, Taylor, Viollett, Pegg. Sub: Charlton
2. **Tottenham** (1960–61)
   Brown, Baker, Henry, Blanchflower, Norman, Mackay, Jones, White, Smith, Allen, Dyson, Sub: Medwin
3. **Liverpool** (1987–88)
   Grobbelaar, Gillespie, Ablett, Nicol, Spackman, Hansen, Beardsley, Aldridge, Houghton, Barnes, McMahon. Sub: Johnston
4. **Leeds United** (1968–69)
   Sprake, Reaney, Cooper, Bremner, Charlton, Hunter, O'Grady, Madeley, Jones, Giles, Gray. Sub: Lorimer
5. **Nottingham Forest** (1977–78)
   Shilton, Anderson, Barrett, McGovern, Lloyd, Burns, O'Neill, Gemmill, Withe, Woodcock, Robertson. Sub: Bowyer
6. **Everton** (1962–63)
   West, Parker, Meagan, Kay, Labone, Gabriel, Bingham, Vernon, Young, Stevens, Morrissey. Sub: Harris
7. **Wolves** (1953–54)
   Williams, Short, Pritchard, Wright, Shorthouse, Slater, Hancocks, Broadbent, Swinbourne, Wilshaw, Mullen. Sub: Flowers

8. **Arsenal** (1988–89)
   Lukic, Dixon, Winterburn, O'Leary, Adams, Thomas, Rocastle, Merson, Smith, Richardson, Marwood. Sub: Bould
9. **Manchester City** (1967–68)
   Mulhearn, Book, Pardoe, Doyle, Heslop, Oakes, Lee, Bell, Summerbee, Young, Coleman. Sub: Connor
10. **Aston Villa** (1980–81)
   Rimmer, Swain, Williams, Evans, McNaught, Mortimer, Bremner, Shaw, Withe, Cowans, Morley. Sub: Gibson

I have to admit that sentiment and emotion played a big part in prompting me to select the Busby Babes as representing the best of Manchester United. Anybody who was around at the time of the Munich air disaster will know the devastating impact that it had on Britain – the whole of Europe, even.

They say that everybody remembers what they were doing when John F. Kennedy was shot. The Manchester United air crash had the same lasting shock effect. It happened just a few days before my eighteenth birthday – on my pal Denis Law's 18th birthday, in fact: 6th February 1958. I was six months into my first season as a League professional. When I heard the tragic news it was as if somebody had cut my windpipe. For a few moments I was breathless with shock. In just a few terrifying seconds one of the greatest teams in the history of club football had been wiped out. United players Geoff Bent, Roger Byrne, Eddie Colman, Duncan Edwards, Mark Jones, David Pegg, Tommy Taylor and Liam Whelan were among those killed in Munich on the way home from a successful European Cup quarter-final match against Red Star Belgrade. That horrific incident left me with a deep psychological fear of flying that I have not completely conquered to this day.

My first instinct when selecting my top ten teams was to pick the 1967 League champions as the Manchester United entry. In George Best, Denis Law and Bobby Charlton they had three priceless jewels in their crown: three of my all-time favourite players. But vintage memories of that pre-Munich United team kept coming up from the cellar of my mind and I finally had to concede that the Busby Babes were the better team.

If I close my eyes and concentrate I can see an action replay of them on my memory screen. The Red Devils, swooping smoothly down the pitch with football that was a delight to the eye even for the opposition defenders on the receiving end. Duncan Edwards stands out like a colossus. If there has been a better, more powerful all-round player then I have not had the good fortune to see him. To the right of him, Eddie 'Snake-hips' Colman is all poetic skill. He could have sold dummies to Mothercare with those body swerves of his.

Just behind big Duncan is the commanding figure of Roger Byrne, a left-back by definition but with all the ball control and finesse of a master forward. Tommy Taylor leads the attack with a dash and daring that you don't see from centre-forwards any more, and Dennis Viollett probes alongside him like a quick-on-the-draw gunfighter. Billy Whelan, the Irish Imp, unlocks the defence with neatly placed passes. Johnny Berry is a bag of tricks down the right wing, and over on the left I have a mental picture of Bobby Charlton – a young, blond bombshell of a player – just starting out on a career that was to make him one of the world's best-loved footballers.

I accept that memory can deceive and make moments from the past seem better than they were, but I know my memory is serving me right on this occasion. I have the evidence of the League tables to support me. You don't win a First Division championship by 11 points (in the days when there were two points for a win) unless you have an exceptional team. And you don't retain the title the following season, 1956–57, by eight points unless that team is something very special.

The Busby babes *were* something very special. They were artists; the rest of us artisans. They were a stringed orchestra; the rest of us were buskers. I make no excuse or apology for waxing lyrical. This was the effect that the United team had on anybody lucky enough to see them in action. They made even the most jaundiced football reporters look for new descriptive phrases.

United caught the imagination with the sheer beauty of their football. While Wolves – their big rivals of the period – were kicking and chasing, United were flowing and sophisticated. Wolves played with their heads, United with their hearts.

The really stupefying fact is that at the time when eight of the team perished in Munich the United side were still two or three years short of their full potential. We never saw the best of them.

A beautiful flower had been crushed before it had reached

full bloom, but it had grown and flourished sufficiently for us to know and appreciate that it was impregnated with a touch of magic. I will be accused of hyperbole; of getting carried away in the land of exaggeration and overstatement. But I don't care. The legend of the Busby Babes lives on in the minds and the memories of those lucky enough to have seen them in action.

I cannot think of a better way to close this chapter on the game that I love than by paying tribute to the greatest club side of my lifetime. I played against that United team and I *know* they were something special.

And now it's time for me to switch to another sport. Gum-shield in, seconds out . . . here comes 'Iron' Mike Tyson!

CHAPTER TEN

Tangling with Tyson

This is my 'hall of fame' chapter in which I indulge in the game of selecting my sporting heroes. I have been lucky enough during the two halves of my life to mix with the rich and the famous, the hyped superstars, and the naturally gifted geniuses. One stands out head and shoulders above them all for making an impression on me: world heavyweight boxing champion Mike Tyson. I met him in his training camp tucked away in the Catskill Mountains in New York State during an interview for the *Saint and Greavsie* show, and to say that he was awesome would be an understatement.

Director Ted Ayling and I caught up with Tyson in the small gymnasium above the cop shop in the one-horse town of Catskill where he was doing his away-from-it-all training in preparation for his world title defence against Michael Spinks in Atlantic City. As I watched him belting giant sparring partners around the ring as if they were punch bags, I got the feeling that I would not want to tango with Tyson, let alone tangle with him.

I really felt that I was in the presence of a being from another planet. The first thing that struck me about him was his cliff wallface of a body, and in particular a neck that looked as if it might once have been a smoke stack on a tug. But it was not just his physical appearance that made an impact with me. He had an aura about him that was almost electric, or even atomic. Back in the mid-1960s I had met Muhammad Ali when he was in London preparing for his first fight against Henry Cooper. He too had an aura, but it was one that brought a smile to your face. Tyson brought a chill to the heart. With Ali, you felt you were in the company as much of a great entertainer as a great sportsman. With Tyson, the feeling was more of being close to an unexploded bomb.

I climbed into the ring to chat with him in front of the television cameras. He gave me a fascinating fifteen minute interview during which he playfully patted me in the ribs, and left a small bruise that I wore like a badge of honour. Mike sounded like a surgeon about to perform a cutting operation as he showed me how he went about mounting a body attack. 'The main target areas,' he said as he pushed me into a corner of the ring under a mock (thank God) assault, 'are the liver, the kidney region, the heart, the floating rib, and the abdomen.'

He brought his massive right fist up into my soft underbelly. 'Then there's the solar plexus punch,' he said. 'It was invented by that great English fighter of yours, Bob Fitzsimmons, when he knocked out James J. Corbett to become the world heavyweight champion. It was a remarkable performance by Fitzsimmons because he weighed no more than a middleweight.'

Tyson peppers his conversation with boxing facts. He is a genuine fan of his sport, and a walking record book on its history. I have never spoken to anybody quite like him. He is an uneducated young man from the dead end of Brooklyn, yet he talks like somebody who has swallowed a dictionary. He would not win any prizes in the academic world, but he has street sense of Mastermind proportions.

'I never forget that I came from the streets,' he said as we chatted casually after the cameras had been switched off. 'I go back to my old neighbourhood a lot. It does me good to remind myself where my roots are. Man, they are the toughest streets on God's earth. Everybody has to fight just to survive. I go to prisons and drug rehabilitation centres to try to give people hope. It makes you want to cry to see old friends who failed to beat the trap into which they were born.'

He broke off to throw a volley of punches of frustration at a heavy punchbag that I had tried hitting earlier. I had hardly moved it, but he set it dancing at the end of his fists, hammering it away from him as if it were as light as a balloon.

Mike then returned to his theme as if uninterrupted. 'I could so easily have become one of the beaten guys. I was running wild with the street gangs, and I was either going to end up locked away in prison or dead. I was careless and reckless and just didn't care one way or the other about anything or anyone. Then I got lucky and discovered boxing, and some good people who believed in me. Now when I go back to my old hang-outs, I tell the kids I see on the street corners where I used to mess around and get in trouble, 'Hey, look what happened for me. You can get out, too, if you just work hard enough and believe in yourself.'

I asked Mike about the influence that Cus D'Amato had had on him. Cus, who managed former world champion Floyd Patterson, had taken Tyson under his wing at the age of 14, becoming his guardian so that he could be released from a school for juvenile delinquents. He had died shortly after steering Tyson to within punching distance of the world title, and without seeing him take over Patterson's record as – at 20 – the youngest heavyweight champion of all time. 'I don't think I'll ever really get used to the fact that Cus ain't around anymore,' said Tyson. 'He was like a father to me. He not only taught me about boxing but also about life. Almost everything I know comes from what Cus told me. For instance, he gave me the discipline that was missing from my early life. He used to say that without discipline you're nothing.'

I had opened up a treasure chest of memories for the Iron Man just by mentioning D'Amato's name. 'This was like Cus's home, you know,' he said, waving an arm to indicate the gym. 'It's as if I can see him and hear him just by walking into the place. I can still feel his presence here. I remember standing right where I'm talking to you now when he lectured me about discipline. 'One day,' he told me, 'you'll meet a real tough guy in the ring who will take your best shots and just keep on coming. You must discipline yourself ready to meet that challenge. By showing discipline you won't become discouraged and, eventually, you will beat that tough guy.' And he also told me how I could make fear my best friend rather than my enemy. He said I should think of fear as I think of fire. If you can control fire, it will cook for you and keep you warm. If you can't control it, it can burn everything around you and destroy you. Keep your fear under control and it will become a friend.'

Mike, talking softly and with a slight lisp that did nothing to lessen his menacing appearance, looked around the gym as if half expecting to see the ghost of Cus D'Amato. 'Cus was the wisest man I ever met. I won the world championship for him and it is one of the saddest things of my life that he wasn't there to share the success. I made our dream come true thanks to him. There ain't never a day goes by that I don't think of him.'

As I left the gym and the most magnetic character I have ever met, Tyson said: 'Give my best wishes to Frank Bruno when you get back to London, and tell him to look after himself. I want him after Spinks. I like Frank, but you'd better warn him that I will be full of bad intentions once we are in the ring together.'

It is history that Tyson destroyed Michael Spinks in just 91 seconds. I returned home full of concern for my pal Bruno, and I worked up the courage to tell Frank to his face that he should stay at home rather than climb into the ring with Tyson.

Lovely old Frank laughed away my fear and bet me that he would prove me wrong. We were at Wembley together watching the 1988 FA Cup final, and after Wimbledon had caused one of the upsets of the century by beating Liverpool he said: 'See, Jim. It's the year of the underdogs. I can do to Tyson exactly what Wimbledon have done to Liverpool.'

It was 1989 before Frank finally climbed into the ring with Tyson, and by then the year of the underdogs was over. It was the time of the top dog, but Bruno did better than I dared hope by taking Tyson into the fifth round before getting stopped. At the time that I am putting this book together there is talk of a re-match, but I hope – for Frank's sake – that it never happens. He has already failed to climb the mountain once. I would hate to see him fall off a second time against the most fearsome fighter I have ever seen. The only way I can see Tyson ever getting beaten is by himself and the extraordinary life he leads outside the ring. He is in total control and free of pressure only when the bell goes to signal the first round of a fight. He can handle anything that happens inside the roped square, but it's the outside-the-ring aggravations that can trip him up.

The most worrying thing I heard about him is that he had turned to the bottle to blot out the worries of marital, managerial and legal writ problems. Nobody finds answers at the bottom of a glass, only more problems.

Talking of boxing and the world heavyweight championship triggers a memory that always makes me chuckle. Muhammad Ali had just defended his word title with a points victory against Ernie Terrell. During a viciously one-sided contest Ali – who had just recently changed his name from Cassius Clay – kept baiting the outclassed Terrell by saying: 'What's my name?'

On the Saturday following the fight I was playing for Spurs against Fulham at White Hart Lane when my team-mate Terry Venables got involved in a bout of fisticuffs with Fulham defender Fred Callaghan. It was pat-a-cake stuff, and as Venners and Callaghan – both from my old manor of Dagenham – stood sparring with each other a voice from the terraces pleaded: 'For Gawd's sake, Tel, tell him your name . . .!'

The referee didn't see the joke and sent them both off. It's a funny old game.

No sporting hero is greater in my estimation than the classics master Lester Piggott. There was nobody who could get within a furlong of him as the greatest jockey of my lifetime, and probably of all time. I wanted to scream when Lester was put behind bars for diddling our best friend, the Taxman. I kept my tongue on a tight rein, hoping to hear somebody from racing come forward and protest about the sad injustice of it all.

But all those people who helped him get lost, confused and suffocated in a money maze kept as quiet as a grave, protecting themselves and their ill-gotten gains. He was left to carry the can not only for his own crime, but also for all those others who get involved in the business of brown-envelope deals. I considered it an absolute disgrace that the establishment chose to make an example of Lester as a warning to all the duckers and divers in the often shady sport of racing. What about all those owners and trainers – real dark horses – who paid him all the undeclared money? Surely they were accomplices.

Let me stress that I do not condone what Lester did. Anybody who fiddles on his scale deserves to be punished. But you don't need to be a Sigmund Freud to appreciate that Lester's miserly hoarding was more the action of a muddled rather than a criminal mind. His defence lawyer put this point in court, but it did nothing to save Lester from a devastating jail sentence. I wonder if the jury in Lester's case would have been more sympathetic had he been as articulate as comedian Ken Dodd, who I was delighted to see walking from the court a free man after his battle with the tax man.

We will never see the likes of Lester in the saddle again. He rode more Derby winners (nine in all) than anybody else, and notched more classic victories (28 in all) than any rider in the history of racing. Along the way he made so many sacrifices, including living on a starvation diet, that he had to concentrate his mind on something to stop himself from going crazy. He chose money. It became his God and, ultimately, was the cause of his downfall after a riding career that will never be approached, let alone equalled.

What was gained by sending him to prison? It will have done nothing to stop the exchanging of brown-paper packages among an element of the racing fraternity who deal in slush money. This kind of transaction has been going on since time immemorial and it will never be stopped. I have had involvement in racing as a part-owner of horses (I've owned a hoof of one and the fet-lock of another) and I know the hey-diddle-diddling that goes on.

They took away Lester's pride, his dignity, his freedom and – good riddance – his OBE. The punishment he should have been given was a suspended sentence, and the sort of fine that would have paralysed his pocket. To lock him away was, to my mind, more criminal than anything Lester had done, and I would have been ready to lead a march on Downing Street to protest at his treatment.

I aired these views at the time, and Susan Piggott, wife of the king of jockeys, contacted me to say how overwhelmed she was by the public response to the great man's crisis. Susan, a real heroine for the way she carried on training Lester's string of thoroughbred horses during his enforced absence from their Newmarket stables, told me before a crashing fall that put her into hospital: 'Lester and I really appreciate your comments, and I am glad to say you are not the only one supporting him. We have had literally thousands of letters and messages of support from people we have never met in our lives before. It has been of tremendous help and comfort during a trying time.'

The Piggotts are not the sort of family to seek sympathy. They have battled through their crisis because they have enormous strength of character, and at the end of the day nothing will be allowed to cloud the fact that Lester remains the greatest jockey ever to climb on a horse. That's something they can never take away from him.

I would liked to have seen the people in racing stand up and be counted. For a start, they could – even now – name the Epsom finishing stretch 'The Piggott Straight.' Let the great man know he remains a hero in the sport that he graced with his skill and daring for nearly 40 years. He has paid his dues. Now racing should pay its respects.

So far the sound of silence from the people in racing – particularly those who helped get him in trouble – has been deafening. And also sickening.

In cricket, the player I most admire is I. T. Botham. I joined him on a leg of his John O'Groats to Land's End charity walk and got a close-up view of the effort he puts in helping those less fortunate than himself. Yet to read some of his press cuttings you would think he was one of the most evil men ever to set foot on a sportsfield.

Botham's private life is continually under the microscope, when the only thing that should concern the media are his performances on the cricket field. There has not been an England all-rounder to touch him in my lifetime, and the only player he would need to bend the knee to is the king of Barbados, Sir Garfield Sobers.

Just one day on the road with Both during his across-Britain charity walk knackered me, but the big feller was already planning to walk in Hannibal's footsteps across the Alps in the company of elephants. For his charity work alone he deserves hero status. I rate Botham a giant among men. Okay, he sometimes lives life on the wild side when he is away from the cricket field. But you cannot expect him to be like a lion at the wicket and then pussyfoot around off the pitch.

I am such a Botham fan that when we got a couple of rabbits as pets for the grandchildren we named them Mr Botham and Mr Gooch. About a week after we had got them we returned home one evening to find a litter of rabbits in the hutch. 'Mr' Botham had been more of an all-rounder than we thought. They were quickly renamed Mr Gooch and *Mrs* Botham.

The tennis player I have always rated above all others is Rod Laver, the Rockhampton Rocket. I play left-handed like him, but there the similarity ends. I have never seen a more accurate placer of the ball than Laver, and I am sure he would have seen off the modern giants like John McEnroe, Jimmy Connors, Ivan Lendl and Boris Becker. The one player who might have given him trouble is the Swedish ice man Bjorn Borg.

British tennis is a sick joke, and it amused me during the last Wimbledon wipe-out to hear one so-called expert saying that the reason Britain cannot produce championship challengers is because of our wet climate.

Doesn't it rain in Germany (Becker and Steffi Graf), Sweden (Borg, Wilander, Edberg) and Czechoslovakia (Lendl, Martina Navratilova, etc)?

I am beginning to wonder – almost seriously – if we should give tennis the elbow at international level and look on it as a spectator sport.

What we have to do is sink all those millions that Wimbledon makes each year in to creating a network of outstanding indoor courts which can be used free of charge by anybody under the age of 20, no matter from which walk of life. Tennis in this country still has the image of being a middle-class pastime, and if you ever bump into any of the blazered old buffers at the All England Club you will quickly understand why. If we want to compete – and win – at the top we must start casting the net among the inner-city areas. It would be a great PR exercise for a sports manufacturer to dish out hundreds of free rackets and balls to deprived kids. We then might find the hungry players who have the urge to play but lack the vital facilities. I have played tennis all my sporting life, and one of the first things I try to organise when I move to any new home is the laying of a court (in Cornwall, we didn't even have time to lay a carpet!). The only way to conquer the game is to concentrate on the three Ps – Practice, Practice and Practice.

It is only by getting it right at grassroots level that we will possibly one day groom the players who can pump the pride back into our game. Until that happens we will have to concentrate on eating the strawberries and cream and leaving the prizes to others.

One quick tennis story: Ion Tiriac, the gifted Rumanian player who helped shape Ilie Nastase into a world-class performer before becoming manager of Boris Becker, was famed on the world tennis circuit for his strength and daring. He had been a physical training instructor in the army, drove in the Monte Carlo Rally, and once punched a hole in a locker-room door when in a rage following a defeat in Paris. His reputation for being wildly eccentric increased in 1970 when he calmly ate a wine glass at a post-tournament banquet, a crunching performance that he is always happy to repeat on request. He became known as the player who could win the crunch points!

Anyone for tennis?

I enjoy watching both Rugby Union and Rugby League. My favourite Union players have been those Welsh wizards Gareth Edwards and Barry John, and the greatest League player I have seen is Ellery Hanley. If there is a better rugby player in the land than Hanley – in either code – then I have not had the pleasure of seeing him.

The way he glided through the match as Wigan walked all over outclassed St Helens in the 1989 Rugby League final was like seeing poetry in motion. I have rarely seen a better balanced runner in all my years connected with the sports world. Pele and Best come to mind, but they did not have to perform their magic under the threat of physical assaults from thumping, full-body tackles (well, not always!).

I enjoy being in the company of Rugby Union players who always have a million anecdotes with which to entertain you. The Irish stories are always the best, like the one about international stand-off Mick English, who was asked to explain how he had managed to miss a vital tackle on England's Phil Horrocks-Taylor during a match at Twickenham. 'Well it was like this,' said Mick with a straight face, 'Horrocks went one way, Taylor went the other and I was left holding the hyphen.'

The all-time master of wit is Dr A. J. F. (Tony) O'Reilly – no relation – who was the pin-up idol of Irish rugby before working his way up the business ladder to the powerful role as chief executive of Heinz. This is one of Tony's typical yarns: 'We were always devising plans to reduce England's home advantage at Twickenham. One I remember was sending a misshapen Irish front row forward, looking like Quasimodo with a ball tucked up the back of his shirt, into the England dressing-room at what we knew would be the peak moment of a call to arms by skipper Eric Evans. Just as Eric was giving his final harangue – 'Remember Waterloo (with an Irish captain), remember Alamein (with another), remember Trafalgar, remember the Armada, remember Agincourt' – our man pushed open the door and said, 'Sorry to be disturbing you, lads, but would any of you be having some hairy twine I can borrow for me boots?' Incidentally, England won the match but we drank them under the table afterwards. So honours were even.'

What a lovely attitude. Those were the good old days when winning wasn't the be all and end all. It's sad to see the win-at-all-costs mentality now even poisoning rugby.

Athletics is not my favourite sport. Running for the sake of it never appealed to me. The closest I've been to a Marathon is eating one. A ball needs to be involved to hold my interest, but I would go a long way to see Sebastian Coe run. He is, without question, the greatest British athlete of my lifetime. Lynn Davies is another athlete who rates high in my list of heroes. I remember being at a *Daily Express* Sportsman of the Year lunch at the Savoy in 1964, just after he had won the gold medal in the long jump at the Tokyo Olympics. Tom Blackburn, of the *Daily Express* read the award winners in reverse order. 'In third place,' he said, 'is Olympic long jump champion Lynn Davies. Unfortunately Lynn cannot be with us today, but we send her our best wishes wherever she may be.'

Poor old Tom could not understand why this was greeted with a gale of laughter. Terry Downes, with a voice that could have carried across the Thames, shouted from a table behind me: 'Send 'er a kiss from me, Tom!'

Finally in my private sports hall of fame is golfer Severiano Ballesteros. Watching Ballesteros against Jack Nicklaus, with both men at peak form, would be my idea of being in a golfing paradise. I love the adventurous way Seve plays the game, and he is never ever dull to watch. I played a round with him in Spain (*what a name dropper you are, Greavsie*) and after watching me slicing the ball off the first tee he said, 'Yimmy, I think you better stick to football.' He then knelt on his knees, took his driver and smashed the ball 250 yards straight down the middle of the fairway.

Max Faulkner, the most colourful British golfing master of them all, is a great raconteur. This is a story he told during a pro-am in my playing days: 'I was teeing off in a domestic tournament when I noticed that my caddie was swaying around like a sapling in a strong wind.

'Are you all right?' I asked.

'I'm as trim as a daisy,' he replied, with a slurred voice.

'You've been at the brandy,' I said.

'That's right,' he slurred. 'And I'll finish off another bottle when you've won this tournament.'

'He followed me down the fairway in a zig-zag fashion. I was on the green in two and putting for a birdie. As I handed him the flag he advised, 'Hit this one slightly straight, sir.'

'I lined up the putt and managed to sink it for my birdie three. When I looked around my caddie was flat out on the side of the green clasping the flag in his arms. I replaced the flag in the hole and then half carried and half dragged him behind a gorse bush where I left him sleeping like a baby. It gave a whole new meaning to being below par!'

And that's where I have to leave the funny old world of sport, because Alf Garnett is waiting to surface.

CHAPTER ELEVEN

The angry old man

Greg Dyke, the man who opened doors into television for me at TV-am before becoming the big white chief at London Weekend, has got the fastest tongue in the west. He is always quick on the draw and shoots from the lip. 'You, Greavsie,' he says, 'have become a real-life Alf Garnett. Why are you so bloody angry all the time?'

Dykie was referring to my appearances on TV-am in the role of television previewer, the job that he kindly gave me. Among the many shows that I have slaughtered are quite a few commissioned by Greg for LWT. I've developed into a Frankenstein's monster that he created, and there are plenty of people gunning for me throughout ITV for bad-mouthing their programmes. I'm sorry, but all I can do is tell the truth – and the truth is that much of what is on offer on television is a load of tripe.

When I was starting out in football John Osborne was making the headlines as 'The Angry Young Man' following the enormous success of his mould-breaking play *Look Back in Anger*. According to Greg Dyke, I am now developing into 'The Angry Old Man' of television.

Yes, I am an angry person when I see things that are not right. And there is a lot that is not right about our television service.

My Alf Garnett-style anger on TV-am has been aimed at the likes of the Met Office (they couldn't tip rubbish), prancing Julian Clary (with fans like him, Joan Collins must wonder who needs enemies), the Queen's honours list (it's a fixed gong show that has become dishonoured), motorway maintenance (they've turned the M25 into the biggest car park in the world) and our lawn tennis authorities (upper-class twits who are more interested in being seen at Wimbledon and getting stuck into the champagne and strawberries than giving deprived kids the chance of playing the game).

But it's my sweeping criticism of the television output that has given me my Alf Garnett reputation. There are influential people in the network who think that because I am appearing on a commercial channel I should confine my comments to boosting ITV programmes. But I see myself as a guide for the viewers, and – leaning heavily on the advice of the knowledgeable Joe Steeples – I feel they deserve to know what is best to watch regardless of the channel that it's on.

I also made enemies across the channel at the BBC when I fired a broadside at *EastEnders*. Speaking as an East Londoner, I know that the programme gets about as close to capturing the real East End as I have got to Mars. Where's the humour for which the real East End is famous? In Mike Reid they have got one of the funniest comedians in the country, but the second he arrived in Albert Square he became just as big a whinger as the rest of the cast. I sense a left-wing tug to many of the storylines as if the production staff are trying to get across a political message, and it's mostly gloom and doom. You can always get a chuckle out of *Coronation Street*, but *EastEnders* leaves you feeling as depressed and washed out as a cat in a spindryer. Off the top of my head I recall their themes including rape, gay rights, homelessness, drug abuse, attempted murder, protection rackets, suicide, family debts, robbery, divorce, infidelity, bastard babies, racial discrimination, wife beating, alcoholism, nervous breakdowns, unemployment, imprisonment, abortion, pornography; the usual everyday life of city folk. I know there are a lot of injustices and hardships in the world, but 7.30pm on BBC is not the time or the place to sort it all out. Somebody with a bit of clout at the Beeb should remind the producers that *EastEnders* is a soap opera, not a soap box.

All right, Alf. Get off YOUR soap box!

The newspapers joined in my *EastEnders* bashing, and *Sun* television critic Garry Bushell tracked down that master scriptwriter Johnny Speight – the creator of my alter ego Alf Garnett – who backed my view with typical crushing humour. 'If *EastEnders* is true to life,' roared the former East London docker, 'then Labour MP Claire Short is a Page 3 girl!'

I made myself less than popular within ITV when I described their output as a load of tripe. I was hitting out at the wall-to-wall repeats, and it is my honest view that unless there is a big re-think on the part of the programme planners there will be a mass exodus of viewers once the satellite companies become established. I am not against all repeats. You cannot see classics like *The Forsyte Saga*, *Upstairs Downstairs*, *Brideshead Revisited* and *Fawlty Towers* too many times. But it is always the rubbish that seems to be continually recycled. Programmes like *The Professionals*, *The Sweeney* and *Bless This House* were just about watchable the first time around, but they are still being screened with that seductive introduction 'another chance to see . . .'

It's my strong belief that the people responsible for what is shown on 'The Box' are not themselves television viewers. They commit the cardinal sin of insulting the intelligence of their audience and have not got a clue what the average punter wants to see. The TV executives live in ivory towers and have as much contact with 'the man in the street' as I have with the Queen Mum. Why don't they introduce a sort of 'taste test' system, inviting ordinary punters to watch previews of programmes that they are thinking of networking? Let them decide whether they are worthy of prime-time screening.

The big bosses – who will no doubt call for my head over some of these comments – will claim that the ratings tell them all that they need to know. Rubbish (or, as Alf Garnett would say, 'do leave orf!'). The ratings might show how many people have got their televisions switched on, but how many of them are *watching* the set? The television is on in my home for hours on end, but half the time nobody apart from the dog is looking at it. 'The Box' is just there to provide background noise, like the way we used to have the radio (or wireless, as we called it) on in the old days. Many of the television companies have a back-up ratings system, with 'audience appreciation' surveys being carried out by teams of canvassers.

But I have had little faith in opinion pollsters since watching an old acquaintance of mine – a part-time canvasser – filling in the forms himself in a boozer where we used to drink and then getting friends to put their names to them.

There are honestly times when I get more enjoyment from watching my fish tank than looking at 'The Box'. Collecting tropical fish has long been a hobby of mine, and I never get tired of looking at them. They are often a lot more entertaining to watch than the tired television programmes.

I caused uproar in the offices of the ITV decision-makers with my comments on TV-am that they are bone lazy, and do not use any imagination when preparing the schedules. TV-am held a phone-in poll to gauge what the viewers thought, and a staggering 98 percent of the callers backed me. The *Sun* held a readers phone-in, asking: 'Do you agree with Greavsie? Are there too many repeats on TV?'

Result: 25,357 people supported my view. Those who voted against: 481.

The *Sun* reported that it was one of the biggest-ever responses to a *Sun* phone-in. Only highly emotive issues like bringing back the rope and tougher sentences for child molesters had generated larger polls.

I am in favour of capital punishment and I would castrate child molesters. Move over Alf Garnett. Greavsie's here!

'This phenomenal support,' said the *Sun*, 'will save Greavsie from a carpeting by TV-am chief Bruce Gyngell.'

But it was Bruce who was on the carpet – rolling about laughing. He thinks it's hilarious when I go into my Alf Garnett act. 'At least people sit up and take notice,' he said. 'The last thing we want to do is bore the viewers.'

That's a philosophy that all television production chiefs should copy.

Adam West – best known as TV's Batman – was sitting alongside me on the sofa when I was knocking the standard of our television programmes. When we were off-camera he told me: 'That's what I call freedom of speech. It would be the quickest way to end a career for an American TV personality to start knocking the goods that his company are offering to the viewers.'

There were plenty of ITV bosses around the country who were thinking along similar lines.

I chuckled. 'Well, Batman,' I said, 'if they sack me I could always get a part with you and Robin . . . as The Joker!'

Now, here comes a commercial break . . .

Often the best things on television, and I mean this most sincerely folks, are the advertisements. I've been lucky enough to feature in several commercials, and they are treated almost as an art form by the talented specialists who make them. There used to be a stigma associated with working on TV commercials. It was looked on as slumming, but now the TV advertising world is a magnet for the best directors and technicians in the business, and the standard of acting is higher than you see in many main productions. Hours of creative thought and energy are poured into producing 30-second masterpieces.

The acting profession used to agree to do commercials only as a last resort. They were considered degrading and detrimental to their careers. But nowadays the finest actors queue for the chance of being featured in a major campaign. The fees are excellent and the exposure does them no harm whatsoever. I defy anybody to pick finer performances on television than those given by Maureen Lipman as the Jewish mum in the British Telecom advertisements, or by George Cole as the Arthur Daley-type spiv in the Leeds Gold commercials. And who can forget the comic genius of Leonard Rossiter, who was always spilling over with enthusiasm in the Cinzano advertisements with Joan Collins; or the classic 'Sch-you-know-who' commercials with William Franklyn that are still fresh in the mind even though the last one was made back in 1974.

One of my favourite commercials in which I have appeared is the one for the Thomson Directory. It is a triumph for the animators who manage to make it look as if I'm having a conversation with Thomson, the cartoon cat. In actual fact I am talking to empty space, with Bill Oddie sitting just off-camera providing the voice for Thomson. I really envy the talent of the artists who produced such a brilliant finished product. My grandchildren are convinced the cat is real and want to know why I have not brought it home.

My easiest appearance was in the Hertz Cars commercial which features The Two Ronnies as rival football managers racing to buy a star footballer. Ronnie Barker wins the race (because he had the good sense to hire a Hertz Car to get him to the football ground to make the signing), while Ronnie Corbett finishes up with two old bangers – a car and me! There was a huge fall of snow just before we made that commercial, and while we were waiting for the Old Trafford pitch to be cleared I sat chatting to the two Ronnies and the other star of the advertisement, England and Manchester United skipper Bryan Robson. Bryan is one of the few players in the modern game who could have stood head and shoulders alongside the giants of my generation, and I had to agree with him that the pressure on modern stars is greater than in my time. For a start there are the all-seeing television cameras that follow their every move on the field (with opinionators like me analysing where they are going wrong) and, much worse, the all-prying reporters who invade their privacy off the pitch. The style of reporting a match and the spotlighting of the behaviour of the players away from the game has changed out of all recognition. In my day they used to write run-of-the-play match reports, but now they tend to concentrate on an individual and cut him off at the legs if he doesn't meet their expectations. After a match the press boys used to beat us to the bar, and we would spend many happy hours together drinking the night away. Now, as Bryan has found to his cost, the top players can find themselves on the front page if they are caught drinking out of hours.

Between takes for the commercial, Ronnie Corbett impressed us with his knowledge of football. His dream had always been to play for Scotland against England as a wing wizard. Ronnie's uncle was an outstanding player with Hearts for whom he had a trial when he was a schoolboy. 'I was told to come back when I had grown a few inches,' he said, 'but I stayed a wee laddie.' Ronnie Barker told me he was going to get out of the business. 'A couple of more smash and grab raids like this (referring to commercials), and that will be it,' he said. 'I've had enough. The time has come to stop and smell the flowers.' I dismissed it as just idle chatter, but within a matter of months he had announced his retirement from all show business work, and I really admire the way he has stuck to his decision. We are left with videos of such series as *Porridge*, *Open All Hours* and, of course, *The Two Ronnies* as a reminder of his genius as a man of comedy.

The scariest commercial in which I have appeared is the one for Dextrasol in which I am shown flying through the air in a rapid sequence of sporting activities, including the pole vault and being thrown like a javelin. I needed to be seen whizzing across the sky, which sounded just the job for a fearless stuntman. But no, it was decided that Greavsie could do it himself. To get the proper effect I had to be lifted 50 feet up in the cradle of a crane where I was fitted with a harness so that I could hang suspended in a horizontal position. I needed a large helping of Dextrasol when that one was in the can!

No question about the funniest commercial in which I have played a part. The Saint and I spent five hours locked into what was unintentionally a sort of Laurel and Hardy sketch while we were making the 30-second advertisement for the Britannia Finance Company.

I was cast as a ruthless, foot-in-the-door, mike-in-the-hand investigative television reporter trying to invade the privacy of a wealthy manor house owner to discover the secret of his riches. The Saint's role was that of a typical English – yes, English – butler. The script called for me to be so wrapped up in talking to the camera that I take a tumble into the swimming pool. Then the Saint, straight backed and immaculate in his butler's uniform, had to haul me out and escort me out of the grounds of the manor. On the way out, me dripping wet, I had to ask him: 'Are you rich?' His response in a snooty voice had to be: 'No, sir, but I intend to be.'

For take after take the Saint failed to satisfy the director with the delivery of his line. He wanted him to sound like Sir John Gielgud in his Oscar-winning role as a butler in *Arthur*. But Ian's Scottishness kept coming through. Just before each take I had a bucket of water thrown over me to give me the drenched, just-out-of-the-pool look. After the fifth take had been declared a no go, I was given the 'sock-it-to-me' water treatment again. Now completely bedraggled, I looked pleadingly at the Saint just before he was about to say his line and pleaded, 'For f***'s sake get it right this time, Saint.' That completely broke Ian up and it was another hour and at least ten more soakings before we finally conquered our giggles and got a perfect take into the can. It was days before I felt properly dried out (and I don't mean that in the way I would have done a few years ago in my drinking days).

The first television commercial in which I appeared, for the Beneficial Trust, was made by Bernie Stringle, the man who directed the documentary *Just for Today* and best known for his skilled work on the award-winning PG Tips advertisements with the chimps. Bernie told me that the first voice-over on the chimp commercial, back in 1956, earned the actor a fee of £100. He was an outstanding impressionist called Peter Sellers. Twenty-three years later Peter was paid £80,000 for a series of commercials for Barclays Bank. Among other famous voices that have been heard on the PG Tips advertisements – the longest running series in Britain – are Stanley Baxter, Fred Emney, Bruce Forsyth, Irene Handl, Kenneth Connor, Arthur Lowe, Bob Monkhouse and Kenneth Williams. They were all paid more than peanuts.

The classic piano-shifting episode featuring the chimps as removal men ('D'you know the piano's on me foot, Dad?' –

'You 'um it, son, and I'll play it.') has been screened more than a thousand times.

As you may have gathered, I have become fascinated by the world of commercials, and I have collected the following facts of which Michael Caine might say, 'Not a lot of people know that . . .'

James Coburn – Our Man Flint – once collected $500,000 simply for saying the words 'Schlitz Light' in a beer commercial in the United States. Actress Faye Dunaway had to work much harder to earn $900,000 for a Japanese TV commercial. She had to say six words!

The most in-demand British celebrity for work in foreign commercials is comedian Benny Hill, who rivals even Margaret Thatcher as the best-known Briton in the world. He appeared in a German beer advertisement in Greece; sold biscuits on television in France; advertised a chain store in Australia; and television sets in Spain. He is continually being bombarded with 'name your own price offers' to work full-time in the United States where he is known affectionately as 'the dirty old man'.

Gary Myers, the man in black, has been appearing regularly on British television screens since 1968 without saying a word. He is the intrepid stuntman who always delivers the chocolates '. . . and all because the lady loves Milk Tray.'

The most successful theme song for a commercial was written by British partners Roger Greenaway and Roger Cook for Coca Cola. It was recorded by the New Seekers as *I'd Like to Teach the World to Sing* and was number one in the British charts for 21 weeks in the winter of 1971–2.

The Rolling Stones provided the backing music for a Rice Krispies commercial featuring a Juke Box Jury-style panel, and cartoon characters of The Beatles were featured in the 1963 advertisement for a Nestlé's chocolate bar.

I reckoned that one of the most compelling advertisements in the early days of commercial television was the one for Strand cigarettes in which a man in a trench coat and with a hat stuck casually on the back of his head, Sinatra-style, wandered through darkened, deserted streets. He then stopped beneath a lamp-post and lit a cigarette. Then up came the simple slogan, 'You're never alone with a Strand'. In the background we could hear haunting music played by composer Cliff 'Sing Something Simple' Adams and his orchestra. The record of the theme music went into the charts and the advertisement was the talk of the nation. Only one thing was wrong: not enough people bought the cigarettes, and the brand was killed off.

Cliff Adams and Johnny Johnson are renowned as the most prolific jingle writers for British commercials. Johnson combined with lyricist Mo Drake to produce what is considered the most catchy jingle of them all: 'A million housewives every day/pick up a tin of beans and say/Beans Meanz Heinz.'

Hercules, a 54-stone circus bear, has become a legendary figure in the world of commercials. He was taken to the Outer Hebrides in the summer of 1980 to be filmed water skiing during the making of an advertisement for toilet paper. He was insured for £500,000 and was treated like royalty with the best steak, scampi, prawns and fish for his meals. But Hercules was unimpressed by all the hospitality. Halfway through the filming he disappeared into the heart of the island and the army had to be called in to find him. He was on the run for 22 days before being shot with a tranquilliser dart. There was so much worldwide publicity that Hercules was invited to the United States where he appeared in cabaret and on chat shows.

That's the end of the commercial break. Now I shall let others do the talking . . .

CHAPTER TWELVE

The things they say

I have tried hard not to make this too much of a football oriented book (or even a Leyton Orient book). Thanks to my new career in television there are a lot of people who do not even associate me with the game that was once my life. Just recently I had a request from a TV-am viewer for an autographed picture of me from my playing days. 'I just want to prove to my son,' he wrote, 'that you actually played the game. He thinks of you purely as a TV celebrity, and had no idea that you were once an England football star.' His son is fifteen, and it makes me aware that there is a whole generation growing up who have no idea of my footballing (or drinking) past. And that's the way it should be. It's today's footballers who deserve the hero status, not mouldie oldies like me.

But I don't want to close my book without bowing the knee to a game that remains the greatest sport ever invented. It is just some of the people in it – violent players, negative coaches, megalomaniac managers, blind referees, selfish chairmen, short-sighted authorities and terrace thugs – who scar the game. Since switching to journalism just over ten years ago (I have my NUJ card to prove I am one of *them*!) I have been collecting the things that people say about football for a sporting quotes book that I hope to have published at some stage. Here is just a sample of some of the wise, witty, wonderful and weird things that have been said by people involved in the greatest game on earth:

"Football is not a game for jokers. If any of my players were to start acting like clowns I would arrange their transfer to a circus."

***Bill Shankly**, late, great manager of Liverpool*

"Football is about reality. It's not about fairy tales like Fleet Street would have you believe."

***Bill Nicholson**, my old boss at Tottenham*

“I'll tell you what football is. It's a rat race. You'll find rats everywhere – in the boardroom, in the dressing-room and, yes, in the manager's chair.”

Tommy Docherty, *that man of many clubs*

“I've had more clubs than Jack Nicklaus, but the difference is that I've always had to carry my own bag. My handicap has been having to pick too many footballers who don't know one end of a football from the other.”

Tommy Docherty, *comical after-dinner speaker*

“Football is like a religion to me. I worship the ball, and I treat it like a god. Too many players think of a football as something to kick. They should be taught to caress it and to treat it like a precious gem.”

Pele, *arguably the greatest player that ever lived*

“No matter where I go in the world I find there is one international language that everybody understands. It's called *football.*”

Sir Stanley Matthews, *The Wizard of Dribble*

“Football in England has become a grey game, played by grey footballers and watched by grey people.”

Rodney Marsh, *before going to the United States*

“A million quid for Mark Hateley? But he can't even trap a dead rat.”

Stan Bowles, *commenting on a transfer story*

“I always say that to maintain interest in sport it is important never to meet sportsmen.”

Roy Hattersley, *deputy leader of the Labour Party*

“I always say that to maintain an interest in politics, it is important not to meet politicians.”

Jimmy Greaves *(I just wanted to reply to Mr H!)*

“Many of the world's greatest entertainers have changed in those Palladium dressing-rooms, but I was disappointed by them. They put me in mind of the dressing-rooms at Hartlepool.”

***Chris Waddle,** the £4 million footballer, talking after his singing appearance with Glenn Hoddle on* Live at the London Palladium

"I don't want to be remembered as the gentleman of football. I would much rather people say 'he could play a bit'."

***Bobby Charlton,** who could play a bit and was also a gentleman of the game*

"No matter what I do in life I will never find anything to match scoring goals. I fed on goals. Every time I put the ball into the net it was ecstasy. Goals were like a drug."

***Brian Clough,** a master at the goal-scoring game*

"I like footballers who don't think about what they're doing. I want them to play naturally. It's when footballers, even the great ones, start thinking about what they're doing that they suddenly can't do it as well."

***Malcolm Allison,** the ace of coaches*

"I've had defenders say to me, 'try to go past me once more and I'll break your f***ing leg'. It's the last thing they should say to me because it then becomes like a challenge to me, and I make it my business to try to go past them again and again."

***George Best,** who had the ability to go past any defender in the world – again, again and again!*

"I cannot understand anybody who goes on to a football pitch wanting to do anything but win. Too many footballers seem to think that playing is enough. *Winning* is the only thing that matters."

***Alan Ball,** one of the most competitive of all players*

"Football is a beautiful game. Pity about some of the people in it. I wouldn't treat a dog the way that I've been treated."

***John Bond,** after being sacked as manager of Birmingham City*

"I think football would become an even better game if somebody could invent a ball that kicks back!"

***Eric Morecambe,** the late master of comedy who was a football-daft director of Luton Town*

❛❛Football is the least complicated of all sports. There are only two basic situations. Either you have got the ball or you haven't.❜❜

__Ron Greenwood,__ former England manager, who never made the game sound that simple when he was giving a pre-match tactics talk

❛❛All you have to do as a manager is keep saying, 'We'll win it . . . we'll win it . . . we'll win it.' Eventually your players will believe you, and they'll go out on to the pitch and win the game for you.'❜❜

__Ally McLeod,__ former Scotland manager talking before the 1978 World Cup finals. His players could not have been listening to him!

❛❛I felt like a circus act when I was playing in America. Roll up, roll up, roll up to see the greatest one-eyed goalkeeper in the world.❜❜

__Gordon Banks,__ talking about his career in the United States where he played for two seasons after a car crash had robbed him of the sight of one eye. Even with one eye he was voted 'most valuable' goalkeeper in the North American League.

❛❛I wouldn't wish some sections of the press on my worst enemies.❜❜

__Bobby Robson,__ when being crucified as England manager

❛❛Norman Hunter telephoned me once to say that he'd gone home with a broken leg. I asked him, 'Whose leg is it?'❜❜

__Les Cocker,__ late Leeds United and England trainer

❛❛I never used to worry about whizzing into a bend at 100 miles an hour, but the prospect of having Norman Hunter coming in to tackle me would frighten the life out of me.❜❜

__Barry Sheene,__ motor cycling ace

❛❛I've got a little black book in which I keep the names of all the players that I've got to get before I pack up playing. If I get half a chance they will finish up over the touchline.❜❜

__Jack Charlton,__ making a statement on television that got him into big trouble with the football authorities

"When I leave home for a match I don't say I'm going to *play* football. I say that I'm going to work."

Mike England, *one of the great centre-halves*

"I am no longer a footballer. I am an industry."

Johann Cruyff, *after a transfer from Ajax*

"When I left school my final report said that I was wasting my time dreaming of becoming a professional footballer. But dreaming never did anybody any harm."

Gary Lineker, *England's goal-scoring hero*

"I believe that it's more than mere coincidence that players in the Stanley Matthews, George Best, Bobby Charlton mould have become extinct since the coaches took over our game."

Denis Law, *saying exactly what I believe*

"A reporter asked me if I took my teeth out to make myself look more ferocious and frightening to opponents. I said, 'No, it's because I don't fancy swallowing my false teeth.'"

Nobby Stiles, *The Toothless Tiger*

"My happiest days were when I was playing at Newcastle United. We all got the same money, and it was a team game in the best sense of the word. It's just not the same now. Too many people with no real ability or feeling for the game are taking too much out of it and putting little back. What they pay some players and managers these days is obscene. They will bleed the game dry."

Bob Stokoe, *former North East playing idol, talking after retiring from management at the age of 55*

"Our match plan is a quite simple one. We always set out to equalize first."

Danny Blanchflower, *the word master blinding the press with Irish science during Northern Ireland's march to the 1958 World Cup quarter finals*

"A lot of people thought I was just a slippery Cockney boy with a few jokes. It has taken one of the biggest clubs in the world to acknowledge what I can do."

Terry Venables, *while manager at Barcelona*

"Football in Spain reminds me of how the game used to be in England about 25 or 30 years ago. There's good-natured banter, happy families strolling to big matches without any fear, children getting excited. You see kids on their father's shoulders and fans proudly wearing the rosettes of their clubs. It sickens me to think the hooliganism in the English game has ended so much of that."

Allan Harris, *talking when No 2 to Terry Venables in Barcelona*

"That Cookie! After he had sold one of his dummies the crowd used to have to pay to get back into the ground."

Jim Baxter, *on Charlie Cooke's dribbling skills*

"That's just about the funniest thing I've ever shaun or heard!"

Bobby Moore, *after Alf Ramsey had thanked 'Seen' Connery for showing a squad of England players around the Pinewood studios during a break in the 1966 World Cup finals*

"I would give my right arm to play for England."

Peter Shilton, *when overtaken by Ray Clemence as England's No 1 choice goalkeeper*

"You get to wish that they would just occasionally pass the ball to the other team, like the rest of us do."

Graham Taylor, *when manager of Watford after they had been beaten by Liverpool in an FA Cup tie*

"I have not enjoyed my football in recent years. There is too much tension and pressure around. It is no longer a sport, but more like a business."

Pat Jennings, *the world's No 1 goalkeeper putting into words the thoughts of many colleagues*

"Football is the only thing that matters in life. I'll die happy if we are 3–1 up at half-time, and happier still if it's 4–0. All the talk of a Super League is for the top boys and the top brass. They want a supermarket. I prefer a corner shop – that's us in the Fourth Division. I'm happy here, working with decent people and gates of 3,000. I can go for a pint anywhere in this town and feel welcome."

Ian Greaves *(no relation), while the manager at Mansfield Town*

"I took the FA Cup home and slept with it."

Peter Osgood, *after he had helped Southampton beat Manchester United in the 1976 FA Cup final*

"Managing Manchester United is both the best and the worst job in the world. It's a magnificent club and you feel that you are in charge of something very special, but when results don't go your way you find out what pressure really means. Manchester suddenly shrinks to the size of a village and you know what everybody is saying about you. One half of the city – the blue half – hates you because you're manager of Manchester United, the other half – the red half – hates you because the team is losing."

Ron Atkinson, *after being succeeded at Old Trafford by Alex Ferguson who soon found out exactly what he meant about the pressure of being United's manager*

"I'll take you to where I used to live in the North-East and show you where I headed a tennis ball so many times against a brick wall near our house that it's got a hole in it. The street I grew up in is 120 yards long and there used to be three games going on at once – promotion, relegation and all. Now you wouldn't see a single kid in the street. It's full of cars. It's amazing we produce any players at all. What are we going to do about it?"

Bobby Robson, *England manager, on the disappearance of the back-street footballers*

"I am being crucified in the newspapers for leaving Jimmy Greaves out of the team, but the truth of the matter is that he's asked not to be considered again for England."

Sir Alf Ramsey, *explaining when manager of England why he had not recalled me after I had hit a purple patch in 1968, a year after my final international appearance*

The actual truth was that I had asked Alf not to select me if he was not going to play me. The last thing I wanted was to join the squad for pre-match training and then be left on the sidelines. I have deliberately closed this quotes section with the comment from Ramsey because it gives me the chance to nail a lie about Alf and me. After he had left me out of the 1966 World Cup final it got about that Alf and I didn't like each other. As a player, I don't think I produced enough perspiration for his liking. But away from the pitch he and I always hit it off.

The private Alf Ramsey was a much nicer, warmer person than the one who appeared in public as always tight-lipped and unsmiling. I don't think he was overproud of his Dagenham background. I came from the same manor (Hainault to be exact), and with the best will in the world I cannot say it's the greatest place on God's earth. But it used to be home to me and I had no hang ups about saying that I came from there. But Alf got moving in circles where backgrounds seemed to matter and it suited him to give the impression he was in no way inferior to the posh-speaking FA councillors and League club directors with whom he mixed.

He started to talk as if he had a plum in his mouth after elocution lessons, but so bloody what! It's no crime to try to improve yourself, and I rate Alf much higher than those allegedly superior twits he was trying to impress.

In his unguarded moments Alf could 'eff and blind' with the best of us, and I've seen him give the old gin and tonics a good seeing to in his relaxed moments. His one major failing was an inability to communicate with the media and the public, particularly if they came from anywhere outside England. He had an inbuilt suspicion of foreigners and a low opinion of many media men. His great strength was his ability to win the absolute loyalty of his players with whom he never had any communication problems.

Alf, for all his la-di-da accent, could never escape from his background as a player, and he was always happiest at the training ground or in the dressing-room. A test of his standing is to go and ask any of the players capped during his reign for an assessment of Alf, and you will find very few with anything less than complete admiration for him as a manager and as a man.

I rate him head and shoulders above any other England

manager, with Bobby Robson second in my ratings and Walter Winterbottom third. I have a lot of affection for Alf despite the fact that he left me out of the one match that I wanted to play in more than any other – the 1966 World Cup final. Let's be honest, it was a brave decision by Alf to leave me on the sidelines for Geoff Hurst, who was relatively inexperienced at international level. If England had lost, Alf would have taken a lot of stick because at the time I was England's leading goal scorer. But Geoff swooped in for his historic hat-trick, and that ended all arguments.

I shall now wind up this football-speak chapter with a quote from me:

"Let the record show that I have no quarrel with Alf Ramsey. In my book, he rates as a master manager."

CHAPTER THIRTEEN

They shoot horses

Now that I have reached the dreaded half century – my 50th birthday passed without celebration on 20th February 1990 – I have to say about my life as I often say about my money: 'Where has it all gone?' The one thing that I cannot get used to is the speed with which life races by. Was it really twelve years ago when I hit rock bottom as an alcoholic, scrambling on my knees alongside a dustbin in the early hours of a winter's morning? I was trying to recover a bottle of vodka that Irene had thrown away in a desperate but hopeless attempt to stop me drinking.

Where did the first half of my life go? Was that really me who they used to call the 'Goal King' because of the ease with which I was able to pump the ball into the net? It must have been because I've got a yellowing newspaper cutting with a banner headline shouting GOAL KING GREAVES. I have just blurred memories of it all, and I feel as if I have been on the outside looking in at somebody else's life.

What I say to outstanding modern players like Gary Lineker, Paul Gascoigne, Bryan Robson, Ian Rush and John Barnes is, as the old song goes, *Enjoy yourself, it's later than you think.* Suddenly, and I promise you that it's in a blinking of an eye, you will find your careers are over. What you must do is recall the past with pride, suck every experience you can out of the present and make sensible plans for the future.

You might think this is Greavsie the insurance salesman talking, but I cannot stress strongly enough to today's players the need to get the best possible guidance on how to invest their money while their earning power is at its peak (and, unashamedly wearing my insurance hat, I will be happy to give 'best advice' to anybody who contacts me). I occasionally see old footballing mates – internationals as well as the bread-and-butter players – on their uppers, and there is little sadder than the old footballer with nothing to kick around but his memories. As I said to George Best when I was struggling to adjust to retirement: 'They shoot horses, don't they. So why not shoot old footballers?'

'Have another drink,' said George. 'And while you're about it, make mine a large one.'

Bestie. What a character. What a player. What a man. What a boozer!

You will find me in philosophical mood in this final chapter of the trip through what has so far been a hectic second half to my life. There is nothing like galloping middle-age to concentrate the mind on making sure you avoid committing any more mistakes in the minefield of life. I have trodden on quite a few mines in my time, but luckily I have remained in one piece.

[*You're never going to believe this, but as my writing partner Norman Giller was typing that last sentence on to the computer screen who should come into the office but our mutual mate Reg Gutteridge, ITV's respected Voice of Boxing. Reggie looked at the screen and said, 'That's a bit strong, lads. You're taking the piss out of me.' Reggie really did step on a mine during the Normandy landings of 1944 and lost the lower part of a leg. 'I played a bit part in* The Longest Day,' *is one of his million jokes. Reggie, from a famous boxing family, was an outstanding junior champion, and he had the courage and character to start a new life after the premature end to his war and his boxing career. He switched to writing and rabbiting about the sport he knows so well after what he called 'a knock out in round one by A. Hitler.' Right, back to the book . . .*]

What I missed most of all when I stupidly retired from football at 31 was being centre stage. Thank God (and Gary Newbon, Bruce Gyngell, John Bromley, Bob Southgate, Bob Burrows, Roy Bottomley and Uncle Tom Cobblers and all), television put me back in the spotlight. All right, sometimes you cannot tell the difference between the real Greavsie and my Spitting Image puppet, but at least I'm up there getting my fat face and refined voice noticed. I promise you that there is nothing more frustrating than being an exhibitionist without a platform. It's like being a pianist without a piano, or a painter without a canvas. Or an alcoholic without a drink.

I'll be the first to admit that I have been a jammy sod to have got another showboating career going for me, while many of my old footballing pals have had to settle for mundane jobs.

This is why I stress the importance of forward planning for today's big-earning footballers.

One day – and one day soon – they will discover that the oil well they have struck has dried up. When they have fired their final shots they will find that there is room for only a handful to continue to make a living out of the game in the managing/coaching field. And the likes of the Saint and I, giggly Emlyn and Bob 'The Headmaster' Wilson will not easily give up our studio seats (mind you, after reading this book, my TV bosses might kick me out to make way for somebody a little easier to handle).

I am building up to a lecture because I am concerned about the stories I hear about many of our current leading players. They have not learned from my mistakes and are, so I am reliably informed, hitting the bottle in spectacular style. They might think they have got it under control, but suddenly – and it creeps up on you like an invisible snake – they will find it is they who are under control of the demon drink.

There is an established England international player who I am told gets paralytic after most matches, and the kitty for the drinking school that he leads is the equivalent of what I used to earn in a week as a First Division footballer. I've been down that road, lording it at the bar after matches and contenting myself that I would be able to run the booze off in training. But please, lads, take it from me – and pin this on the dressing-room noticeboard – **BOOZERS ARE LOSERS.**

Maybe they see me on 'The Box' and think that I have done all right for myself despite swimming in alcohol during and immediately after my playing career. What they haven't seen is the torture that I went through in the days when I was being haunted by the dreaded DTs. You have no doubt heard of James Stewart and his imaginary friend Harvey, a giant rabbit, when he was playing the part of an alcoholic. Well in my nightmares I was accompanied by an anything-but-friendly giant in a suit of armour. He used to threaten to crush me in the desperate days when my drinking was out of control. In my sober moments I was able to identify him as the foot-tall figure in armour that decorates our fireplace to this day, but in my drinking fits he used to look eight foot tall and was a terrifying sight as he came menacingly towards me.

I have suffered the terrible indignity of being strapped to a hospital bed to stop me from doing myself an injury when my drunken rages were pushing me to the edge of suicide. I am not reliving these memories for the sake of sensation (I've had enough sensation to last me a lifetime, thank you). I am recalling the horrors that I went through in a sincere attempt to try to convince any of today's footballers – anybody, for that matter – that they should drink only in moderation.

It is not necessarily the heavy drinkers who get themselves trapped by the illness of alcoholism. I was not the biggest drinker in my school. Bobby 'Old Hollow Legs' Moore could drink me under the table. So could indestructible Dave Mackay and Alan 'Make mine a double' Gilzean. And I was always running a bottle of champers behind Malcolm Allison when we used to hit the London clubs (and I don't mean Arsenal, Spurs etc). But all four have come through their boozing without bruising.

I had lower resistance to the advance of alcoholism, and when I realised the danger it was too late. I was trapped into that nightmare world in which one drink is too many and twenty is not enough. To all those footballers – people from any walk of life – who are saying, 'It couldn't happen to me' think again. It *can* happen to you unless you drink sensibly. The moment you *have* to have that next drink, you are in trouble.

To all footballers my message is: Please take it easy. There is nothing wrong with a pint or two as reward and relaxation after a match or a tough training session. But know when to say no to the next round. I have had the stories from enough sources to realise the extent of the drinking – and even some drug taking – on the footballing circuit. It honestly worries me, and if this chapter pulls up any of the lads and makes them control their drinking then old Greavsie, recovering alcoholic, will be delighted.

Now it's Grandad Greavsie talking. I am concerned about the world we are creating for my grandchildren ... *all* grandchildren. I worry about the way our planet is being polluted ... I worry about what they're doing to our food ... I worry about the ozone layer ... I worry about the dangers of drug abuse ... I worry about the spread of AIDS ... I worry about the way our green and pleasant land is disappearing under an ocean of cement ... I worry about nuclear waste. Yes, I've become an old worry guts, and with good reason.

The Green Party have got too many cranky notions for me

to take them too seriously, but they have done the country a big favour in making environmental issues a major talking point. If the two premier parties are too thick to realise the concern running through the minds of millions of people then the Greens could find themselves lifted to a seat of power by worry-gut grandparents like Irene and me.

I have always been a political animal (right of Genghis Khan, Greg Dyke would say). But while I am a Tory with deep socialist roots, I would not hesitate to switch my allegiance to the party that can promise to make the environment number one on their manifesto. Now that I am well into the second half of my life I want to encourage the powers-that-be to create a better world than the one I entered in 1940. When I was born in East Ham a maniac with a toothbrush moustache was preparing to unload his bombs on London. I had entered a world at war. Now my grandchildren are being born into a world losing a war against pollution.

Before I bow out I would like to see the world a better place. For the sake of my grandchildren, and their children, and their children's children. If we are not careful there will not be a world for them to inherit. I think there is a lot of worrying coming my way. A funny old life?

What shall I be doing the rest of my life? I would like the opportunity to add the role of Greavsie the Gardener to my television output. Put me in a garden and I am a contented man, and I have got ideas how to put over gardening advice that will appeal to the ordinary dig-and-plant man. I would also like a crack at a different type of chat show in which I literally stop 'the man in the street' and just rabbit to him on any given subject. Everybody has got a tale to tell, and I would jump at the opportunity of interviewing ordinary people and finding out their stories. I am sure it would be more fascinating than talking to so-called celebrities. But something I have learned about the world of television is that you don't shape it as much as it shapes you. I have had several offers from independent companies with satellite TV contracts, but at the moment I am content ploughing the conventional network field. How much longer I can survive in the television jungle is the $64,000 question, particularly with regimes changing as the commercial companies brace themselves ready for the franchise revolution promised for the future. As Sam Goldwyn once said, 'It's a dog eat dog world, but nobody's going to eat me!'

Much of my future energy is going to go into building up my insurance business with my daughter Lynn, who has got her mother's practical mind thank goodness. Just twelve years ago I did not think I had a future. Now I want to encourage people to build for it with wise investment and winning policies. One thing I will not be doing is becoming a member of the 'smart set'. In the summer of 1989 I was voted one of Britain's seven scruffiest men. I was in good company. The other 'seedy' six – according to the Mr Harry menswear chain – were Terry Wogan, Jeremy Beadle, Kenny Everett, Gorden Kaye, Nigel Lawson and Neil Kinnock. Scruffiness makes strange bedfellows! I like to think of myself as casual smart. I have always hated wearing ties and would like to strangle the man who invented them, using a Windsor knot of course. I am happiest in an open-necked shirt and a sweater (provided it's not endorsed by Emlyn Hughes).

On the writing front, Norman Giller and I are already plotting our fourteenth book together. It is a novel focusing on the two worlds that I know best – football and television. It will be as realistic as we can make it, but we shall be changing most of the names to protect the guilty. Here, provisionally, is how the novel starts . . .

> *Groves started the second half of his life the way he had finished the first, in a position that was all too familiar: on his knees, head over the toilet and being as sick as a dog. It was the spring of 1990 and he was about to make his first public appearance since admitting that he was an alcoholic. Downstairs in the London Weekend Television Studio Michael Aspel was waiting to interview him on* Aspel and Company. *Upstairs Groves was throwing up. It's a funny old life!*

Or maybe that is too far fetched for a novel.

Also in the second half of my life I must find as much time as possible for Irene, the lady without whom there would – for me – be no television career, no books, no insurance company, no future. I owe her everything, and I have got to try to make up for the years of happiness that she lost because of my slavery to the bottle. That's the worst thing about alcoholism. It is those nearest and dearest to the alcoholic who suffer the most.

Somehow I must find a way to make amends. Somehow.

On reading back all the things I have had to say in the previous pages I have been concerned that the material is too self indulgent, but the Publisher – he who must be obeyed – put my mind at rest by pointing out that it is rather difficult to write an autobiography 'without talking about one's self.' It's a fair point. I am also worried that anybody reading about my Jekyll and Hyde personality might send for the men in the white coats, but I am not really that bad provided I can choose which sweater to wear. There is no truth in the rumour that I'm playing the lead in *Psycho IV*.

I finish my book as I started: on my knees, not being sick this time but saying a silent prayer of thanks to 'the greater power' for getting me into the second half of my life in reasonable shape considering the liberties I have taken with my body and my brain. If there is anybody left out there, I thank you for having stayed to the final whistle. Perhaps we'll meet again in extra time?

I'll leave you with this thought: *It's a funny old life!*

APPENDIX ONE

An A to Z of TV

I feel that the thing lacking in awards shows is a booby prize category. We are always being told about the best things on 'The Box' but nobody ever stands up and says, 'and now, the nominations for the *worst* performance of the year on television are . . .' For instance, I could have at least got a nomination for my early performances on my chat show series when I was stumbling around the kitchen set as if I had drunk the wine meant for the *coq au vin*.

On the following pages I give an A to Z breakdown of what I consider has been the best *and* the worst on television.

For the top shows and performers I award the **Greavsie Gold**, and for what – in my opinion – are the flops I award the **Greavsie Core**.

There are quite a few golden oldies (and some mouldy oldies) scattered through my selections, and I have restricted my nominations to the last twenty-five years. One other rule, in case you want to play the game, is that I have allowed myself a maximum of five nominations for each award.

So here we go . . . lights, music, opening titles. It's. . . .

THE BEST
AND THE WORST
TV AWARDS SHOW...

The nominations for the ***Greavsie Gold*** *are* Alan Alda (*for his cutting lines in M*A*S*H*), All Creatures Great and Small (*everybody's pet series*), Michael Aspel (*with his red book*), The Avengers (*with Patrick MacNee keeping tongue in cheek and umbrella at the ready as Steed*) *and* Auf Wiedersehen Pet (*for building laughs*). *And the winner is...*

AUF WIEDERSEHEN PET. This brought new height, breadth and depth to television comedy. A typical joke: Oz walks into an Indian restaurant in Dusseldorf, looks around misty eyed and says in his thick Geordie accent: 'Aye, man, this place makes me really home-sick for Gateshead.'

The nominations for the ***Greavsie Core*** *are* The Adventures of Dick Turpin (*even Black Bess was off colour*), Airwolf (*it made me airsick*), All Gas and Gaiters (*it was enough to give you an allergy to the clergy*), Are You Being Served (*leant too heavily on limp-wristed John Inman and pussy jokes*), *and everything* Australian (*apart from Bruce Gyngell, Richie Benaud and Clive James*). *And the losers are...*

THE AUSSIES. I feel sure that the likes of *Neighbours, Home and Away, Richmond Hill*, Kylie Minogue and Jason Donovan have been sent over here as revenge for our ancestors shipping all those convicts Down Under.

The nominations for the ***Greavsie Gold*** *are* David Bellamy (*The Botanic Man*), Richie Benaud (*supreme cricket commentator*), The Boys from the Blackstuff (*scorching Scouse humour*), Bread (*more laughs from Liverpool*), *and* Brideshead Revisited (*tales of the toffs*). *And the winner is...*

BRIDESHEAD REVISITED. British acting, writing and directing at its best. The 13-part series quite properly won great acclaim for its two principal stars, Anthony Andrews and Jeremy Irons. Sebastian's teddy bear also deserved an Oscar!

The nominations for the ***Greavsie Core*** *are* The Baron (*it was barren of entertainment*), Michael Barrymore (*for Saturday Night Out*), Blankety Blank (*only Les Dawson saves it from a total blank*), Lennie Bennett (*for the punchless Punchlines*), Bless This House (*it got no better when repeated in 1989*), Max Bygraves (*for Family Misfortunes*). *And the winner is...*

MICHAEL BARRYMORE. Even his bouncing personality failed to save *Saturday Night Out* from being one of the great mish-mashes of our television times. It made viewers wish they were having a Saturday night out whenever it was on.

The nominations for the ***Greavsie Gold*** *are* Cheers (*hilarious life behind bars*), Joan Collins (*our greatest export to the States*), Bill Cosby (*a master of comedy*), Tommy Cooper (*he could trick us into laughter, just like that!*) *and* Coronation Street (*a window on the world of the north*). *And the winner is...*

CORONATION STREET. The soap opera that has been getting to the heart of things for more than a quarter of a century. It remains a street ahead of its rivals without resorting to sensational storylines.

The nominations for the ***Greavsie Core*** *are* Casanova '73 (*an alleged comedy series that was a rare floperoo for Leslie Phillips and master writers Galton and Simpson*), David Cassidy (*I gave him the bird when he was in The Partridge Family*), Celebrity Squares (*the quiz for squares*), Charlie's Angels (*no wonder Charlie never showed his face*), *and* The Colbys (*a soap without any bubbles*). *And the loser is...*

THE COLBYS. It was a spin-off from *Dynasty*, and quickly spun off our television sets. The only magnetic attraction was Charlton Heston's hairpiece. He could have negotiated a sponsorship deal with Axminster.

The nominations for the ***Greavsie Gold*** *are* Dad's Army (*on parade for vintage comedy*), Dallas (*cowboys and gindians and the well-oiled JR*), *any one of the* Dimblebys (*a family at jaw*), Sir Robin Day (*without question, the king interviewer*) *and* Judi Dench (*there ain't nothin' like this Dame*). *And the winner is...*

SIR ROBIN DAY. One of the great sights over the last quarter of a century has been that of politicians squirming in their seats while being interrogated on TV by the reliant Robin. He is a boa constrictor in a bow tie, and has been a good knight heard by all.

The nominations for the ***Greavsie Core*** *are* Dempsey and Makepeace (*cops and sobbers*), Don't Forget to Write (*a rare miss for George Cole*), Charles Drake (*not for me, my darlings*), Dukes of Hazzard (*stock car racing with dialogue*), Dynasty (*I prefer Dysentery*). *And the loser is...*

DEMPSEY AND MAKEPEACE. It should have been retitled Dumbo and Makeweight. There was violence for the sake of violence, and storylines that were so far fetched that they were often lost in the world of fantasy. A poor rip-off of American models.

The nominations for the ***Greavsie Gold*** *are* Edward VII (*a royal treat from Timothy West*), Michael Elphick (*for Private Schultz, Boon and Three Up, Two Down*), Emmerdale Farm (*the soap that has a field day*), Edna Everage (*housewife megastar who is never a drag*), Ever Decreasing Circles (*superb suburban humour*). *And the winner is...*

EMMERDALE FARM. It has believable storylines, strong characters, a beautiful setting and humour mixed in with the pathos. It is a sort of Yorkshire (rather than Mrs) Dales diary; the Archers of 'The Box.' You can almost smell the fertilizer.

The nominations for the ***Greavsie Core*** *are* EastEnders (*a soap that gets in the eyes*), Ellis Island (*sunk without trace*), Erik Estrada (*I was hoping to see him get his chips in CHiPs*), Eurovision Song Contest (*I'll give it deux points*), Linda Evans (*it was her unlucky destiny to finish up in Dynasty*). *And the winner is...*

EASTENDERS. It started full of bright promise, but got lost in a maze of misery. When Dirty Den and Angie were at each other's throats, the action was at least gripping. The producers should take lessons from *Brookside* about how to show life as it really is.

The nominations for the ***Greavsie Gold*** *are* Peter Falk (*for giving style to the dirty mac brigade*), Fawlty Towers (*five star humour in a one-star hotel*), A Fine Romance (*Michael Williams with punch and Judi*), The Forsyte Saga (*the grand-daddy of dramas*), *and* David Frost (*he's always welcome*). *And the winner is...*

FAWLTY TOWERS. A towering, maniacal performance by John Cleese, with marvellous support from Prunella Scales, Connie Booth and Andrew Sachs. They did not provide bed and breakfast as much as bedlam and breakfast.

The nominations for the ***Greavsie Core*** *are* The Fall Guy (*Lee Majors could not make me fall for this plastic American stunt series*), Fame (*some great music and dance, but the storylines were too contrived and cringey*), Family Fortunes (*relatively awful*), Fantasy Island (*I've had more entertainment on the Isle of Dogs*), *and* Michael Fish (*'There will be no hurricane'*). *And the loser is...*

FAMILY FORTUNES. How this so-so show survived the disastrous season with Max 'Big Money' Bygraves in charge I'll never know. They should have laid it to rest when original question master Bob Monkhouse switched channels.

The nominations for the ***Greavsie Gold*** *are* Bamber Gascoigne (*University Challenge, reading question cards*), The Glittering Prizes (*which graduated with honours*), The Golden Girls (*22 carat comedy*), The Good Life (*for The Good Laugh*) *and* Alec Guinness (*for sheer genius*). *And the winner is...*

SIR ALEC GUINNESS. His performances as spycatcher George Smiley made *Tinker, Tailor, Soldier, Spy* and *Smiley's People* riveting television and revealed just why he is rated one of the all-time great actors.

The nominations for the ***Greavsie Core*** *are* Game for a Laugh (*a pity viewers didn't enjoy it as much as the presenters*), Jill Gascoigne (*brilliant in The Gentle Touch, but not in C.A.T.S. Eyes*), The Golden Shot (*missed the target with me*), Goodbye Mr Kent (*a rare flop for Hannah Gordon and Richard Briers*) *and* Jimmy Greaves (*for his chat show*). *And the loser is...*

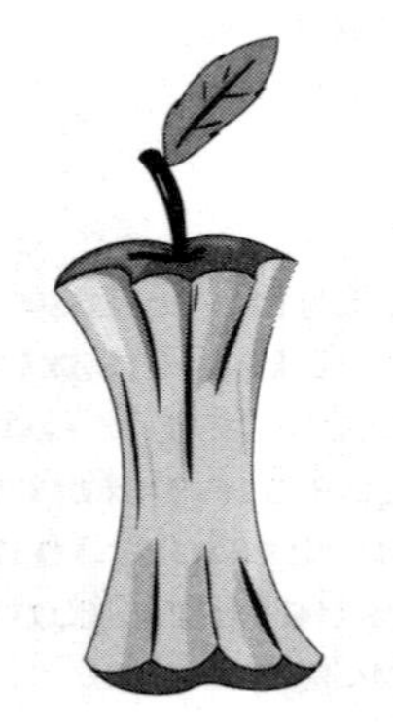

JIMMY GREAVES. In accepting this coveted award I would like to thank all those people who helped me make a twit of myself in my chat show series. I found out that talking's easy. It's the listening that's hard.

The nominations for the ***Greavsie Gold*** *are* Larry Hagman *(for being the best baddie on TV)*, Benny Hill *(like Heinz, he has made a fortune from sauce)*, Bernard Hill *(for Yosser 'gissajob' Hughes)*, Hill Street Blues *(an all-action station), and* Howard's Way *(Dallas on the Solent). And the winner is...*

HILL STREET BLUES. It brought quality to cop shop programmes, with an exciting cocktail of human drama, comedy, street crime, romance, aggro and intrigue. *The Bill* has successfully copied the formula.

The nominations for the ***Greavsie Core*** *are* Hadleigh *(fine at the start but ran out of steam)*, Hard Cases *(failed its probation)*, Keith Harris *(I would like to see Emu and the awful Orville fight to the death)*, Highway to Heaven *(pass the Kleenex? No, the sick bag), and* Hollywood Wives *(Tinseltown tittle tattle). And the loser is...*

HOLLYWOOD WIVES. Never in the history of television has so much talent been wasted on so few decent lines. It was take-your-money-and-run time for a string of stars headed by Rod Steiger, Angie Dickinson, Stefanie Powers, Robert Stack and Anthony Hopkins.

The nominations for the ***Greavsie Gold*** *are* I Claudius (*with a st-st-staggering performance by Derek Jacobi*), Inspector Morse (*arresting stuff*), Jeremy Irons (*for Brideshead*), Ironside (*thrills on wheels from Raymond Burr*), *and* It Ain't Half Hot Mum (*how we won the war!*). *And the winner is...*

INSPECTOR MORSE. ITV had the courage to give two hours to each episode, and thanks to an exceptional performance by John Thaw in the title role (supported by Kevin Whately) the series never dragged for a single second.

The nominations for the ***Greavsie Core*** *are* In Loving Memory (*I was always waiting for Thora Hird to sing songs of praise*), The Incredible Hulk (*he didn't grow on me*), John Inman (*for Take a Letter Mr Jones*), Interceptor (*hell with a helicopter*), The Invisible Man (*I couldn't see anything in it*). *And the loser is...*

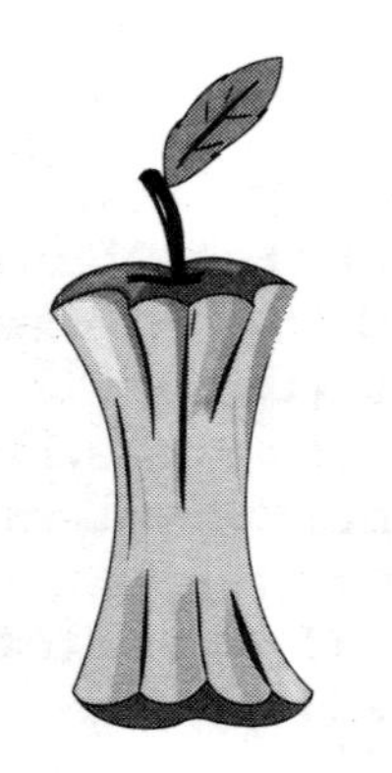

INTERCEPTOR. A sort of poor man's *Treasure Hunt*, with Anabel Croft as the shrieking presenter. The ideas should have been intercepted at birth. With *Treasure Hunt* we at least had Anneka Rice and Anabel showing off their greatest assets.

The nominations for the ***Greavsie Gold*** *are* Glenda Jackson (*for Elizabeth R*), Clive James (*proving that not all Aussies have their brains in a beer can*), Derek Jameson (*I gave him elocution lessons*), David Jason (*a delight as Delboy*), The Jewel in the Crown (*a real gem*). *And the winner is...*

THE JEWEL IN THE CROWN. The jewel in the crown of ITV, and a triumph for the drama department of Granada. It rivals *Brideshead Revisited* as the finest production in world television in the last 25 years.

The nominations for the ***Greavsie Core*** *are* Jenny's War (*made me want to escape from the telly*), David 'Kid' Jensen (*for The Roxy, a pop-show disaster*), Don Johnson (*and his designer suits in Miami Vice*), Juliet Bravo (*weak when compared with, for instance, The Bill*), Just Amazing (*oh no it wasn't*). *And the loser is...*

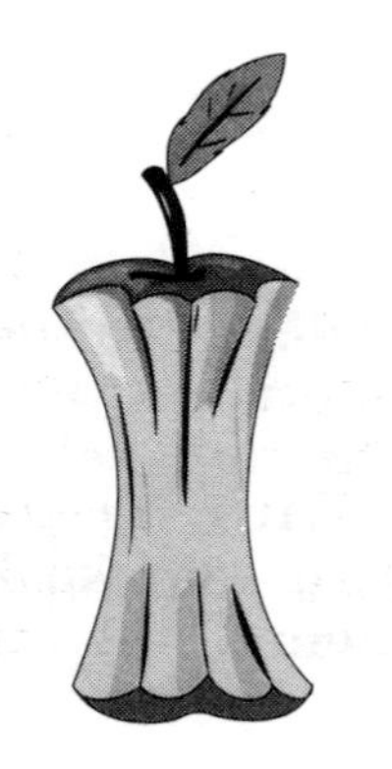

DAVID JENSEN for *The Roxy* which promised so much for pop fans and produced just a load of rubbish. It was supposed to be ITV's answer to *Top of the Pops*, but was so loosely put together that it quickly bombed. Even the younger members of the Greaves clan voted it a miss.

The nominations for the ***Greavsie Gold*** *are* Penelope Keith (*for To The Manor Born*), Felicity Kendal (*for the Good Life*), Jack Klugman (*for Quincy and The Odd Couple*), Kojak (*I loved it, baby*) *and* The Krypton Factor (*one of the better quiz shows*). *And the winner is...*

PENELOPE KEITH. She was marvellous as the snooty Margot Leadbetter in *The Good Life* and there seemed no way she could top it. Then she came up with an even more captivating performance in *To The Manor Born*. She's a Penny from heaven.

The nominations for the ***Greavsie Core*** *are* Keep It in the Family (*they can keep it*), Henry Kelly (*for going on and on in Going for Gold*), Graham Kerr (*The Galloping Gourmet who would not get within miles of Keith Floyd*), Knight Rider (*a nightmare*), *and* Knots Landing (*the poor man's Dallas*). *And the loser is...*

KNIGHT RIDER. A car that talks, thinks and is indestructible. It might just have been all right for the kids' schedule, but this was bought from America with an adult audience in mind. It was an insult to the intelligence.

The nominations for the **Greavsie Gold** *are* Angela Lansbury (*for her Miss Marple-ish detecting in Murder She Wrote*), Last of the Summer Wine (*vintage comedy getting better with age*), Life on Earth (*earth moving*), The Likely Lads (*a comedy feast from the North-East*), *and* Maureen Lipman (*it's never agony watching her*). *And the winner is...*

LIFE ON EARTH. Sir David Attenborough's fascinating account of how all the living species arrived on earth was both enlightening and entertaining. Attenborough always holds the attention and puts real life into his presentations.

The nominations for the **Greavsie Core** *are* Lace (*would not even have made a decent pair of curtains*), Life Begins at Forty (*a comedy series?*), The Little and Large Show (*in need of new material*), Little House on the Prairie (*Yuk!*), *and* Desmond Lynam (*for being smug*). *And the loser is...*

LIFE BEGINS AT FORTY. Oh no it didn't! It was a lifeless series. Watching David Nimmo changing nappies did not make exactly riveting television. I've had more entertainment watching the test card.

The nominations for the **Greavsie Gold** *are* Magnum (*champagne stuff from Tom Selleck*), M*A*S*H (*a smash*), Minder (*hilarious Cockney capers*), Monty Python's Flying Circus (*took over where the Goons left off*), *and* Morecambe and Wise (*out on their own*). *And the winner is...*

MINDER. George Cole's portrayal of the conniving Arfur Daley (with magnificent support from Dennis Waterman) is so sharp you could cut your fingers on it. Even though he's nagged by 'er indoors, the world is still his lobster!

The nominations for the **Greavsie Core** *are* Ali MacGraw (*for Winds of War*), Man from Atlantis (*it met a watery grave*), Master of the Game (*an all-star cast for a load of rubbish*), Miss World (*in reverse order, the plastic parade*), *and* Patrick Mower (*for missing the target in Target*). *And the loser is...*

MAN FROM ATLANTIS. Patrick Duffy did well not to sink out of sight in this load of rubbish about a swimmer with webbed hands and webbed feet. He surfaced to make a splash in *Dallas,* and has proved that oil and water *do* mix.

The nominations for the ***Greavsie Gold*** *are* The Naked Civil Servant (*John Hurt in Crisp form*), John Nettles (*puts the sting into Bergerac*), News at Ten (*slick and authoritative*), Paul Nicholas (*for Just Good Friends*), *and* Barry Norman (*and why not, indeed!*). *And the winner is. . .*

BARRY NORMAN. He previews the films for BBC with a beautiful turn of phrase, and knows his subject inside out. Each of his *Hollywood Greats* series has been a real eye-opener. He never hogs the camera or the microphone at the expense of the subject.

The nominations for the ***Greavsie Core*** *are* Name That Tune (*I'm not keyed up for this quiz show*), Never the Twain (*antique jokes*), New Faces (*where are they?*) Barry Newman (*for being too clever by half as Petrocelli*), *and* Nine to Five (*not a patch on the film*). *And the loser is. . .*

NEW FACES. What ever happens to all those acts that we are told are going to be the new stars of tomorrow? It's the same old faces who keep popping up on the screen, which is proof that this discoveries show (like *Opportunity Knocks*) does not come up with much-needed new talent.

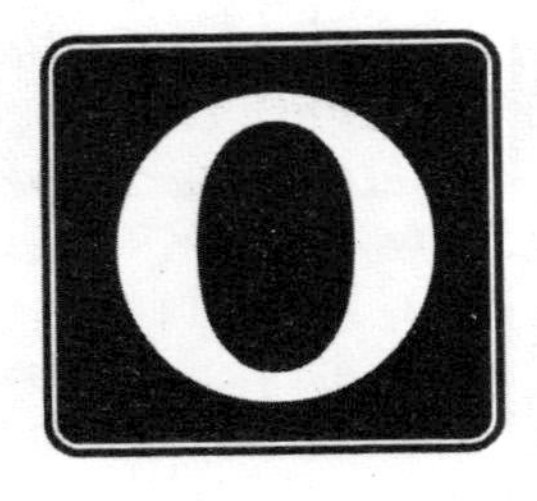

The nominations for the **Greavsie Gold** *are* Bill Oddie (*for proving there is life after The Goodies*), Laurence Olivier (*for Voyage Around My Father*), Omnibus (*an arts programme that does not bore*), Only Fools and Horses (*side-splitting spivvery*), *and* Open All Hours (*A Ronnie B-B-Barker classic*). *And the winner is...*

ONLY FOOLS AND HORSES. This is comedy-off-the-back-of-a-lorry as provided by ace script-writer John Sullivan. His cracking lines are delivered perfectly by David Jason (Delboy), Nicholas Lyndhurst (Rodney) and Buster Merryfield (Uncle Albert).

The nominations for the **Greavsie Core** *are* Ian Ogilvy (*Ian St John makes a better Saint*), Only When I Laugh (*it was just about funny the first time around, but all the repeats have damaged its health*), Opportunity Knocks (*it's time the door was closed*), Donny Osmond (*and/or Marie Osmond*), *and* The Other 'Arf (*was only half right*). *And the losers are...*

THE OSMONDS. The Marie and Donny show was just about the most plastic ever imported from the USA, and that's saying something. It was like a never-ending advertisement for dental treatment.

The nominations for the ***Greavsie Gold*** *are* The Pallisers (*a classic costume drama*), Panorama (*at its best when Richard Dimbleby was the anchorman*), Michael Parkinson (*the king of chat*), Pennies from Heaven (*acting and music to remember*) *and* Porridge (*another great vehicle for Ronnie Barker*). *And the winner is...*

PORRIDGE. It would almost be worthwhile being locked up if you could get a cellmate like Ronnie Barker in his role as the cunning and comical Norman Stanley Fletcher. Fulton Mackay, Brian Wilde and Richard Beckinsale gave marvellous support. My life behind bars was never this funny!

The nominations for the ***Greavsie Core*** *are* Planet of the Apes (*silly monkey business*), Play Your Cards Right (*with Bruce Forsyth as the joker in the pack*), Police Woman (*Angie Dickinson looked pretty in a pretty awful series*), The Price is Right (*Come on down? No thank you*) *and* The Professionals (*it was repeated to death*). *And the loser is...*

THE PRICE IS RIGHT. The idea of the game is a sound one, but I was turned off by seeing the audience whipped into a Yankee-style frenzy. The producer was William G. Stewart, who made amends by bringing us one of the best quizzes on television in *Fifteen-to-One*.

The nominations for the ***Greavsie Gold*** *are* Q.E.D. (*detailed documentaries as only the Beeb can do them*), Anthony Quayle (*for Great Expectations and The Last Days of Pompeii*), A Question of Sport (*consistently entertaining*), Question Time (*Robin Day's asides made it watchable*), Quincy (*medics and murder*). *And the winner is...*

A QUESTION OF SPORT. It has been the number one sports quiz show for more than a decade. *Sporting Triangles* still has some way to go to catch it up. I thought it was at its best when big Billy Beaumont and wee Willie Carson were the rival captains, and I always liked their sweaters!

The nominations for the ***Greavsie Core*** *are* QB VII (*not a patch on the Leon Uris book*), Quatermass (*lost in space*), Queenie's Castle (*lovely Diana Dors labouring with a Yorkshire accent*), A Question of Sex (*Clive James and Anna Raeburn did not come up with satisfactory answers*) *and* Quiller (*disappointing spy series*). *And the loser is...*

QUATERMASS. Anybody who recalled the original *Quatermass* adventures on BBC in the 1950s will have voted this 1979 revival a miss. Thames brought *Quatermass* back to our screens. They should have left it in the pit.

The nominations for the ***Greavsie Gold*** *are* Rising Damp (*Leonard Rossiter lording it as a sly landlord*), Robin of Sherwood (*Take a bow Michael Praed and Jason Connery*), Rumpole of the Bailey (*courtroom chuckles*), *and* Anton Rodgers (*for Fresh Fields*). *And the winner is...*

RUMPOLE OF THE BAILEY. The adventures at the bar (both legal and liquid) of the acid-tongued Rumpole makes this courtroom comedy-drama a twin triumph for roly poly actor Leo McKern and witty writer John Mortimer. Rumpole's formidable wife – 'she who must be obeyed' – adds to the fun.

The nominations for the ***Greavsie Core*** *are* Esther Rantzen (*for That's Life*), Remington Steele (*over-acted, over-rated and over here!*), Return to Peyton Place (*nowhere near as good as the original*), Joan Rivers (*Can we talk? No!*), *and* Roots (*it just didn't take root with me*). *And the loser is...*

ESTHER RANTZEN. As presenter of *That's Life* she is too toothy and toothsome for my taste. The show lost all its snap when Paul Heiney and Chris Serle departed. I much preferred this sort of consumer guidance programme when it was under the eagle eye of Bernard Braden.

The nominations for the **Greavsie Gold** *are* Soap (*a send-up of all soaps*), Some Mothers Do 'Ave 'Em (*Michael Crawford as the king of the wallies, Frank Spencer*), Sesame Street (*streets ahead in the educational scene, and it brought us The Muppets*), Spitting Image (*making dummies of everyone*), *and* Star Trek (*for gripping space adventure*). *And the winner is...*

STAR TREK. The voyage of the Starship Enterprise around the planets has logged hours of entertainment for viewers. William Shatner and Leonard 'Ear Ear' Nimoy head a highly professional cast who have made it a cult show. Beam me up, Scottie!

The nominations for the **Greavsie Core** *are* Scarecrow and Mrs King (*I would rather watch Worzel Gummidge*), Sorry! (*Ronnie Corbett was great in the first series, but it went on too long*), The Saint, (*No, not my partner but the programme*), Richard Stilgoe (*too clever by half*), *and* The Sullivans (*a cardboard soap from Down Under*). *And the loser is...*

THE SAINT. The series was all right when young Roger Moore had the halo ... so-so when suave Ian Ogilvy took over ... but then a disaster when Simon Dutton landed the role of Simon Templar. The halo hung over his head like a noose.

The nominations for the ***Greavsie Gold*** *are* That Was The Week That Was (*a trail-blazer for satire and sarcasm*), John Thaw (*for Inspector Morse*), Till Death Us Do Part (*Alf Garnett on the warpath*), Tinker, Tailor, Soldier, Spy (*gripping spy serial*), *and* To the Manor Born (*Penelope Keith and Peter Bowles in rich form*). *And the winner is...*

TILL DEATH US DO PART. Alf Garnett is the greatest comic creation of the last thirty years. Through his loud mouth, writer Johnny Speight has been able to gleefully take spiteful swipes at the establishment. Actor Warren Mitchell is moo-sic to the ears as mouth-and-trousers Alf.

The nominations for the ***Greavsie Core*** *are* Ticket to Ride (*I hope it's not a return ticket*), That's Life (*the presenters are always so bloody smug*), Top of the Pops (*the kids deserve better than this tired format*), Triangle (*a North Sea ferry soap that sank out of sight*), *and* Trick or Treat (*tasteless and tatty*). *And the loser is...*

TRICK OR TREAT. Mike Smith and the mincing Julian Clary were co-presenters of a show that should never have reached our screens. It was far too juvenile for adult audiences, and too smutty for children's television.

The nominations for the ***Greavsie Gold*** *are* Upstairs Downstairs (*drama among the masters and servants*), Stanley Unwin (*for his double talk*), University Challenge (*for intellectuals, yet interesting for us plebs*), The Untouchables (*entertaining for the sixth time around!*) *and* Peter Ustinov (*the master raconteur*). *And the winner is...*

UPSTAIRS DOWNSTAIRS. Whether up with the masters or down with the servants, the standard of acting and presentation never slipped below top class. The late, lamented Gordon Jackson served up a procession of outstanding performances as Hudson, the butler.

The nominations for the ***Greavsie Core*** *are* Tracy Ullman (*she has become really cringey since switching to the States*), Ultra Quiz (*a Japanese idea that did not travel well*), The Upchat Line (*John Alderton held it together, but it fell apart when he left*), Up Pompeii (*it was funny at first thanks to Frankie Howerd, but it then became vulgar*), *and* Robert Urich (*for Vegas*). *And the losers are...*

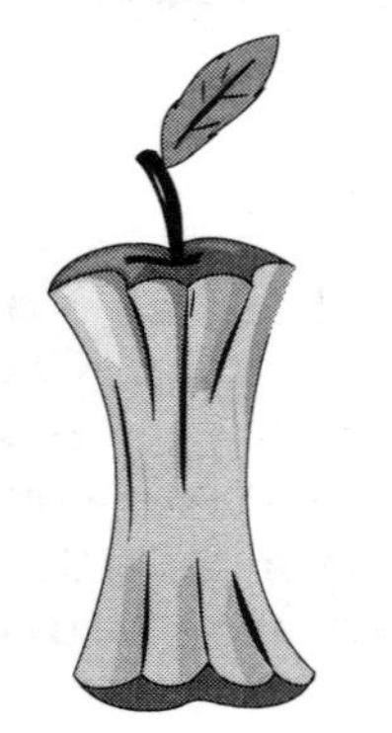

ULTRA QUIZ. One of the few flops that David Frost has been involved with during his full-to-overflowing television life. The Japanese played the elimination game with a ruthless attitude, but we Brits were too gentlemanly and ladylike to make the format work.

The nominations for the ***Greavsie Gold*** *are* 'V' (*V for victory for the aliens*), Van der Valk (*Dutch cops and robbers*), Robert Vaughn (*for Man from UNCLE*), The Virginian (*a superior western series*), *and* A Voyage Round My Father (*the memoirs of John Mortimer*). *And the winner is...*

A VOYAGE ROUND MY FATHER. There have been two versions on TV, but the runaway winner was the Thames treatment of a beautifully written play by the creator of Rumpole. Laurence Olivier, as Mortimer's father who continued as a top counsel despite blindness, gave a performance that revealed just why he was rated The Master.

The nominations for the ***Greavsie Core*** *are* Dick Van Dyke (*for his revived Dick Van Dyke show*), Reg Varney (*for playing the piano and not sticking to the buses*), Vegas (*a loser from the gambling city*), Gore Vidal (*there's never enough room on my set for his ego*), Voyage to the Bottom of the Sea (*it hit rock bottom*). *And the loser is...*

VOYAGE TO THE BOTTOM OF THE SEA. This creation by disaster movie king Irwin Allen started out well enough, but by the fourth season it was scuppered for ideas and credibility. They ran out of storylines down at the bottom of the sea and should have pulled the plug after the second series.

The nominations for the ***Greavsie Gold*** *are* Washington Behind Closed Doors (*cracking Watergate-style drama*), Alan Whicker (*and his fascinating world*), Terry Wogan (*for blarney and cheerful chat*), Victoria Wood (*with or without Julie Walters*), *and* The World at War (*a history masterpiece*). *And the winner is...*

THE WORLD AT WAR. The greatest war history documentaries ever produced, and a lasting testimony to the skill and vision of Jeremy Isaacs as a producer. Every one of the 26 episodes made compelling (and chilling) viewing. Laurence Olivier provided a perfect narration.

The nominations for the ***Greavsie Core*** *are* Lindsay Wagner (*for Bionic Woman*), Kent Walton (*for always wrestling with his words*), June Whitfield (*for going on and on with Terry Scott in Terry and June*), Wings (*a promising series that just didn't take off*), *and* Edward Woodward (*for The Equalizer*). *And the loser is...*

EDWARD WOODWARD. He made his fame and fortune in the United States with *The Equalizer*, which is based on the daft idea of a retired FBI agent settling scores for private citizens. He was much more convincing in his role as *Callan*.

There is only one nomination for the ***Greavsie Gold*** *in this category. And the winner is. . .*

THE XYY MAN. This Granada thriller series featured an ex-crook (played by Stephen Yardley) trying to go straight, but he was plagued by the extra chromosomes which provided the taut series with its title. It was memorable for the support acting of Don Henderson as Inspector George Bulman, who was later given a series of his own.

There is only one nomination for the ***Greavsie Core*** *in this category. And the loser is. . .*

CLUB X. A mish-mash of young talent allowed to go over the top in the area of bad taste because of a lack of direction. They provided a lot to admire, but in one alleged comedy sketch they managed to feature a skeleton purporting to be Eric Morecambe, who had more talent in his little finger than everybody on the show put together. For that alone they deserve the Core.

The nominations for the ***Greavsie Gold*** *are* Mike Yarwood (*always impressive*), Yes, Minister (*Whitehall farce*), David Yip (*for the Chinese Detective*), Susannah York (*for We'll Meet Again*), *and* Robert Young (*for getting plenty of practice as Marcus Welby MD*), *And the winner is...*

YES MINISTER. Nigel Hawthorne just about keeping a civil tongue in his head while bending Minister (and later Prime Minister) Paul Eddington to his will. A funny and often mocking look at the Civil Service, with a lot of truth between the laughter lines.

The nominations for the ***Greavsie Core*** *are* Yanks Go Home (*I wish they had*), Paula Yates (*for The Tube*), Young at Heart (*a weak vehicle for the great talent of Sir John Miles*), The Young Ones (*I was too old to appreciate it*), *and* You're Only Young Once (*Peggy Mount and Pat Coombs up to their ears in corn*). *And the loser is...*

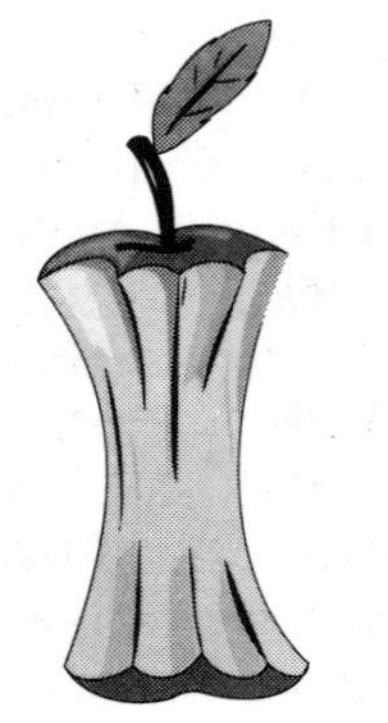

YANKS GO HOME. This 13-part Granada series was a good idea that just did not catch on. The stories of a USAAF base in Lancashire were lacking in reality, and the viewer was unable to warm to the main characters. In short, it bombed.

There is only one nomination for the ***Greavsie Gold*** *in this category. And the winner is...*

Z CARS. It ran and ran for 667 one-hour episodes from 1960 until 1978, and rarely provided anything less than top entertainment. Among the actors who became major stars were Stratford Johns, Frank Windsor, Jeremy Kemp, James Ellis, Brian Blessed and Colin Welland. Of the modern programmes, *The Bill* comes closest to it for atmosphere and reality. It was a trend setter for cop shows, and spawned the spin-offs *Softly Softly* and *Barlow*.

There is only one nomination for the ***Greavsie Core*** *in this category. And the loser is...*

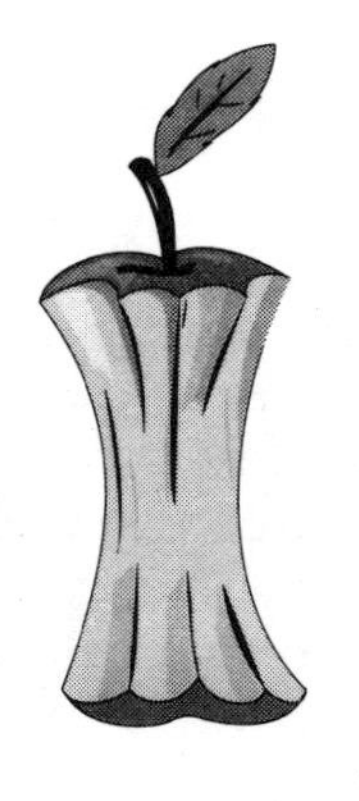

ZOO GANG. No, it was not a wild-life programme but a big budget series about members of a wartime resistance group getting together 30 years later to combat modern crime. Despite an all star cast including Lilli Palmer and John Mills and theme music by Paul and Linda McCartney it failed to capture a following.

Appendix Two

The Greaves File

Compiled by Michael Giller

PERSONAL

Born: East Ham, London, February 20, 1940.

Father: Jimmy senior, a London tube train driver (died August 1989, aged 80). Mother: Mary. Has younger sister, Marion, and younger brother, Paul, both of whom gained teaching diplomas.

Married Irene Barden in 1958. Children: Lynn, Jimmy (dec.), Danny, Mitzi, Andy. Grandchildren: Gemma, James, Louise, Thomas, Victoria, Hannah and Sam.

Education: Southwood Lane School, Dagenham; Kingswood Secondary School, Hainault. Left school in April, 1955, aged 15. He had been 'discovered' by Chelsea football scout Jimmy Thompson.

PROFESSIONAL FOOTBALL CAREER

CHELSEA (1957-1961). The most prolific goal-scoring season of his career was in 1956-57 while still an apprentice professional. He scored 114 goals in youth team matches and Chelsea presented him with an illuminated address to mark the feat.

On August 23, 1957, the first day of the following season, he made his League debut against Tottenham at White Hart Lane and scored.

Between 1957 and 1961, Jimmy scored 124 goals in 157 League games for Chelsea. He was the First Division's top goal scorer in 1958-59 with 33 goals and in 1960-61 with 41 goals.

He scored three or more goals in 13 First Division matches for Chelsea...

4 v. Portsmouth (57-58)
3 v. Sheffield Wednesday (57-58)
5 v. Wolves (58-59)
3 v. Nottingham Forest (58-59)
3 v. Preston (59-60)
3 v. Birmingham City (59-60)
5 v. Preston (59-60)
3 v. Wolves (60-61)
3 v. Blackburn (60-61)
3 v. Manchester City (60-61)
5 v. West Bromwich Albion (60-61)
4 v. Newcastle United (60-61)
4 v. Nottingham Forest (60-61)

Jimmy scored 3 FA Cup goals for Chelsea: 1 v. Newcastle United (58-59); 1 v. Aston Villa (58-59); 1 v. Bradford (59-60). He scored 2 goals in the League Cup for Chelsea: 2 v. Millwall (60-61).

He was sold to AC Milan for £80,000 in June, 1961.

AC MILAN (1961). Jimmy made his debut for AC Milan on June 7, 1961, scoring in a 2-2 draw with Botafogo at the San Siro Stadium. He made 14 appearances for AC Milan and scored 9 goals.

In November, 1961, he was bought by Tottenham for £99,999. Manager Bill Nicholson did not want to burden him with the extra pressure of being British's football's first £100,000 footballer [a distinction that went to Denis Law when Manchester United bought him from Torino for £116,000 in 1962].

TOTTENHAM (1961-1970). On December 16, 1961, Jimmy made his debut for Spurs against Blackpool at White Hart Lane and he scored a hat-trick. Between 1961 and 1970, he scored a club record 220 League goals in 321 matches for Tottenham.

He was the First Division's top scorer a record six times, twice with Chelsea; four times with Tottenham...

1958-59: 32 goals
1960-61: 41 goals
1962-63: 37 goals
1963-64: 35 goals
1964-65: 29 goals
1968-69: 27 goals

Jimmy won two FA Cup winners' medals with Tottenham, against Burnley in 1961-62 (scoring a classic third minute goal) and against Chelsea in 1966-67.

He netted two goals to help Spurs win the European Cup Winners' Cup Final with a 5-2 victory over Atlético Madrid in Rotterdam in 1963.

He scored three or more goals in First Division matches on 12 occasions for Tottenham...

3 v. Blackpool (61-62)
4 v. Nottingham Forest (62-63)
3 v. Manchester United (62-63)
3 v. Ipswich Town (62-63)
4 v. Liverpool (62-63)
3 v. Nottingham Forest (63-64)
3 v. Blackpool (63-64)
3 v. Birmingham City (63-64)
3 v. Blackburn Rovers (63-64)
3 v. Ipswich Town (64-65)
3 v. Burnley (67-68)
4 v. Sunderland (68-69)

Jimmy scored 32 FA Cup goals for Spurs...

3 v. Birmingham City (61-62)
2 v. Plymouth (61-62)
2 v. West Bromwich Albion (61-62)
1 v. Man United (semi-final, 61-62)
1 v. Burnley (Final, 61-62)
3 v. Torquay United (64-65)
3 v. Ipswich Town (64-65)
1 v. Preston (65-66)
1 v. Portsmouth (66-67)
2 v. Bristol City (66-67)
2 v. Birmingham City (66-67)
1 v. Nottm For. (semi-final, 66-67)
2 v. Preston (67-68)
1 v. Liverpool (67-68)
1 v. Walsall (68-69)
1 v. Wolves (68-69)
2 v. Aston Villa (68-69)
3 v. Bradford City (69-70).

He scored five League Cup goals for Spurs: 3 v. Exeter City (68-69); 1 v. Peterborough (68-69); 1 v. Arsenal (68-69).

West Ham United bought Jimmy in March, 1970 for £54,000 as a makeweight in the deal when Spurs signed Martin Peters in British football's first £200,000 trade.

WEST HAM UNITED (1970-71). Jimmy scored two goals in his debut for West Ham United against Manchester City at Upton Park on March 20, 1970. He notched two more goals in the 1969-70 season and netted 9 for West Ham in his final season. In 1971, Jimmy Greaves retired at the age of 31.

ENGLAND. Jimmy scored two goals in his England Under-23 debut against Bulgaria at Stamford Bridge on September 25, 1957 (and missed from the penalty spot).

His 13 goals in 12 England Under-23 international matches is a record.

In his full international debut he scored England's only goal in a 4-1 defeat by Peru in Lima on May 17, 1959.

Between 1959 and 1967 he scored 44 goals in 57 full England internationals. Only Bobby Charlton (49 in 106 matches) has scored more. His goals for England...

1959: Peru (2), Wales (1)
1960: Yugoslavia (1), Northern Ireland (2), Luxembourg (3), Spain (1), Wales (2)
1961: Scotland (3), Italy (1) and Austria (1)
1962: Peru (3), Argentina (1, World Cup finals), Northern Ireland (1), Wales (1)
1963: Czechoslovakia (2), Wales (1), Rest of the World (1), Northern Ireland (4)
1964: Eire (1), Brazil (1), Northern Ireland (3), Holland (1)
1965: Scotland (1), Hungary (1)
1966: Yugoslavia (1), Norway (4)
1967: Spain (1).

Jimmy played his last international match against Austria in Vienna on May 27, 1967. In his 57 international appearances England won 30 games, lost 14 and drew 13.

Jimmy played in 516 Football League matches and scored 357 goals, all of them in the First Division (a record):

Chelsea	**124**	**(1957-61)**
Tottenham	**220**	**(1961-70)**
West Ham	**13**	**(1970-71)**

These are the teams against which he scored his League goals:

Nottingham Forest (24)
Burnley (19)
Blackpool (18)
Wolverhampton Wanderers (17)
Birmingham City (17)
West Bromwich Albion (16)
West Ham United (16)
Leicester City (15)
Manchester City (15)
Blackburn Rovers (14)
Manchester United (13)
Newcastle United (13)
Fulham (12)
Arsenal (11)
Aston Villa (11)
Everton (11)
Liverpool (11)
Leeds United (10)
Preston North End (10)
Sunderland (10)
Sheffield United (9)
Ipswich Town (9)
Sheffield Wednesday (8)
Stoke City (7)
Southampton (6)
Bolton Wanderers (5)
Coventry City (5)
Portsmouth (5)

Tottenham Hotspur (5)
Chelsea (4)
Cardiff City (2)
Derby County (2)
Luton Town (2)
Northampton Town (1)
Leyton Orient (1)
Queen's Park Rangers (1)

His average score per First Division game was .691 and he was leading First Division goal scorer a record six times. He was top scorer for his club in 12 of the 14 seasons in which he played in the First Division.

Jimmy missed five months of the 1965-66 season following an attack of hepatitis that robbed him of half a yard of pace.

At 21, Jimmy became the youngest player to score 100 League goals. At 23 years and 290 days he scored his 200th League goal, which was exactly the same age at which Dixie Dean had reached the milestone with Everton.

He also scored 10 European Cup Winners' Cup goals, 3 in the Fairs Cup, 6 in Inter-League matches, 2 in the Charity Shield, 12 in England Under-23 internationals, 2 for England v. Young England, 2 for the Rest of Europe team and 1 for England v. the Football League.

His total goals in all matches at the time of his retirement in 1971 was 491.

He played non-League football with Brentwood, Chelmsford, Barnet and Woodford Town from 1974 until 1979.

FOOTBALL VIEWS

Most memorable goal: A left-footed scissors-kick in his debut for Tottenham v. Blackpool at White Hart Lane in 1961-62.

Favourite goal by another player: A Bobby Charlton left-foot shot after a thirty-five yard run for Manchester United against Tottenham at White Hart Lane in 1967-68.

Greatest footballing moment: Helping Spurs to become the first British club to win a European trophy – the European Cup Winners' Cup in 1963.

Greatest disappointment: Missing the 1966 World Cup Final when England beat West Germany 4-2 after extra-time [Jimmy played in England's first three matches in the 1966 World Cup finals, and was injured against France. He was not fit for the quarter-final against Argentina and Geoff Hurst took his place and scored the winning goal. Hurst retained his place in the semi-final against Portugal and the final against West Germany, during which he scored the first World Cup Final hat-trick in history].

JIMMY'S FAVOURITE BRITISH PLAYERS
(Against or with whom he played)
Goalkeepers: Pat Jennings, Gordon Banks, Peter Shilton.

Full-backs: Roger Byrne, Ray Wilson.
Centre-halves: John Charles, Roy McFarland, Mike England, Billy McNeill.
Wing halves: Duncan Edwards, Dave Mackay, Pat Crerand. Central defenders: Bobby Moore, Norman Hunter.
Midfield schemers: Raich Carter, Colin Bell, Jimmy McIlroy, Johnny Haynes.
Wingers: Stanley Matthews, Tom Finney, George Best, Jimmy Johnstone.
Strikers: Denis Law, Brian Clough, Roger Hunt.
Centre-forwards: Bobby Smith, Ron Davies, Ian St John, Alan Gilzean.

Favourite captains: Danny Blanchflower, Dave Mackay and Bobby Moore.
Favourite current players: Gary Lineker, Paul Gascoigne, Peter Beardsley, John Barnes.

Favourite managers: Bill Nicholson, Bill Shankly and Brian Clough.

MISCELLANEOUS :

Hobbies: Gardening, keeping tropical fish, driving (Jimmy and co-driver Tony Fall finished sixth out of 96 starters in the 1970 World Cup rally that started in Wembley Stadium and finished in Mexico City).
FAVOURITE THINGS:
Other sports: Tennis, cricket, horse racing (watching, not betting).
Sportsmen: Ian Botham, Rod Laver, Lester Piggott.
TV programme: Fawlty Towers.
TV soap: Coronation Street.
Film: The Godfather.

Actor: Alec Guinness.
Actress: Katharine Hepburn.
Comedian: Eric Morecambe.
Singers: Frank Sinatra, Ella Fitzgerald
Food: Fresh lobster, salad
Drink: Tea, coffee, Perrier water.
Newspapers: The Sun, Daily Mail, Sunday Times.
Authors: Tom Sharpe, Robert Ludlum, Jeffrey Archer.

TELEVISION CAREER

1980-87: Star Soccer (Central)
1981-1987: Greaves Reports (Central)
1982 and 1986: ITV World Cup panellist
1983- : TV-am (as television previewer)
1985- : Saint & Greavsie Show (LWT)
1987- : Sporting Triangles (Central)
1987-88: Jimmy Greaves (chat shows)

BOOKS BY GREAVSIE:
My World of Soccer
A Funny Thing Happened on the Way to Spurs
Let's Be Honest
Two Saint & Greavsie Annuals

BOOKS WITH NORMAN GILLER:
This One's On Me
Stop the Game Ref (I Want to Get On)
GOALS!
The World Cup
Taking Sides
Book of Football Lists
The Final (novel)
The Ball Game (novel)
The Boss (novel)
The Second Half (novel)
Sports Quiz Challenge I
Sports Quiz Challenge II
It's A Funny Old Life

Index

Index